Economy of the Unlost

MARTIN CLASSICAL LECTURES

The Martin Classical Lectures are delivered annually at Oberlin
College through a foundation established by his many friends
in honor of Charles Beebe Martin, for forty-five years a teacher
of classical literature and classical art at Oberlin.

John Peradotto, *Man in the Middle Voice: Name and
Narration in the* Odyssey

Martha C. Nussbaum, *The Therapy of Desire: Theory and
Practice in Hellenistic Ethics*

Josiah Ober, *Political Dissent in Democratic Athens:
Intellectual Critics of Popular Rule*

Anne Carson, *Economy of the Unlost (Reading Simonides
of Keos with Paul Celan)*

Helen P. Foley, *Female Acts in Greek Tragedy*

Mark W. Edwards, *Sound, Sense, and Rhythm: Listening to
Greek and Latin Poetry*

Economy of the Unlost

(READING SIMONIDES OF KEOS WITH PAUL CELAN)

Anne Carson

PRINCETON UNIVERSITY PRESS

PRINCETON AND OXFORD

Copyright © 1999 by Princeton University Press
Published by Princeton University Press, 41 William Street,
Princeton, New Jersey 08540
In the United Kingdom: Princeton University Press,
3 Market Place, Woodstock, Oxfordshire OX20 1SY
All Rights Reserved

Fourth printing, and first paperback printing, 2002
Paperback ISBN 0-691-09175-7

The Library of Congress has cataloged the cloth edition of this book as follows

Carson, Anne, 1950–
Economy of the unlost : reading Simonides of Keos with Paul Celan
/ Anne Carson.
p.   cm. — (Martin classical lectures. New series)
Includes bibliographical references and index.
ISBN 0-691-03677-2 (alk. paper)
1. Simonides, ca. 556–467 B.C.—Criticism and interpretation.
2. Celan, Paul—Criticism and interpretation.   3. Literature,
Comparative—Greek and German.   4. Literature, Comparative—German
and Greek.   5. Economics in literature.   6. Aesthetics.   I. Title.
II. Series: Martin classical lectures (Unnumbered). New series.
PA4411.C37   1999
884'.01—dc21   98-49984

British Library Cataloging-in-Publication Data is available

This book has been composed in Baskerville

Printed on acid-free paper. ∞

www.pupress.princeton.edu

Printed in the United States of America

6   7   8   9   10

ISBN-13: 978-0-691-09175-4 (pbk.)

Contents

Note on Method

Nur hat ein jeder sein Maas.
(*Hölderlin*)

THERE IS too much self in my writing. Do you know the term Lukács uses to describe aesthetic structure? *Eine fensterlose Monade.*[1] I do not want to be a windowless monad—my training and trainers opposed subjectivity strongly, I have struggled since the beginning to drive my thought out into the landscape of science and fact where other people converse logically and exchange judgments—but I go blind out there. So writing involves some dashing back and forth between that darkening landscape where facticity is strewn and a windowless room cleared of everything I do not know. It is the clearing that takes time. It is the clearing that is a mystery.

Once cleared the room writes itself. I copy down the names of everything left in it and note their activity.

How does the clearing occur? Lukács says it begins with my intent to excise everything that is not accesible to the immediate experience (*Erlebbarkeit*) of the self as self. Were this possible, it would seal the room on its own boundaries like a cosmos. Lukács is prescribing a room for aesthetic work; it would be a gesture of false consciousness to say academic writing can take place there. And yet, you know as well as I, thought finds itself in this room in its best moments—

locked inside its own pressures, fishing up facts of the landscape from notes or memory as well as it may—vibrating (as Mallarmé would say) with their disappearance. People have different views on how to represent the vibration. "Names" and "activity" are euphemisms for the work. You may prefer different euphemisms; I

[1] Lukács (1917), 19.

guess the important thing is to copy down whatever vibration you see while your attention is strong.

Attention is a task we share, you and I. To keep attention strong means to keep it from settling. Partly for this reason I have chosen to talk about two men at once. They keep each other from settling. Moving and not settling, they are side by side in a conversation and yet no conversation takes place. Face to face, yet they do not know one another, did not live in the same era, never spoke the same language. With and against, aligned and adverse, each is placed like a surface on which the other may come into focus. Sometimes you can see a celestial object better by looking at something else, with it, in the sky.

Think of the Greek preposition πρός. When used with the accusative case, this preposition means "toward, upon, against, with, ready for, face to face, engaging, concerning, touching, in reply to, in respect of, compared with, according to, as accompaniment for." It is the preposition chosen by John the Evangelist to describe the relationship between God and The Word in the first verse of the first chapter of his Revelation:

πρὸς Θεόν

"And The Word was with God" is how the usual translation goes. What kind of withness is it?

I am writing this on the train to Milan. We flash past towers and factories, stations, yards, then a field where a herd of black horses is just turning to race uphill. "Attempts at description are stupid," George Eliot says, yet one may encounter a fragment of unexhausted time. Who can name its transcactions, the sense that fell through us of untouchable wind, unknown effort—one black mane?

Economy of the Unlost

False Sail

HUMANS VALUE economy. Why? Whether we are commending a mathematician for her proof or a draughtsman for his use of line or a poet for furnishing us with nuggets of beauty and truth, economy is a trope of intellectual, aesthetic and moral value. How do we come to take comfort in this notion? It is arguable that the trope does not predate the invention of coinage. And certainly in a civilization so unconditionally committed to greed as ours is, no one questions any more the wisdom of saving money. But money is just a mediator for our greed. What does it mean to save time, or trouble, or face, or breath, or shoe leather? Or words? His biographers recount that when the poet Paul Celan was four years old, he took a notion to make up his own fairy tales. He went about telling these new versions to everyone in the house until his father advised him to cut it out. "If you need stories the Old Testament is full of them." To make up new stories, Celan's father thought, is a waste of words.[1] This father's sentiments are not unusual. My own father was inclined to make skeptical comments when he saw me hunched at the kitchen table covering pages with small print. Perhaps poets are ones who waste what their fathers would save. But the question remains, What exactly is lost to us when words are wasted? And where is the human store to which such goods are gathered?

There is a poem of Paul Celan that seems to be concerned with the gathering in of certain poetic goods to a store that he calls "you." Among these goods are the lyric traditions of the poetry of courtly love, of Christian mysticism, of Mallarmé, of Hölderlin, not to say Celan himself. Celan has chosen to contemplate these

Fragments of Simonides are cited from the editions of Page (1962) = *PMG;* Page (1981) = *FGE;* and West (1971) = *W.* All translations are my own unless otherwise noted.

[1] Chalfen (1991), 41.

3

traditions through the focusing device of one brilliant and drastic moment from the romance of Tristan and Isolt: the moment of the false sail.[2]

MATIÈRE DE BRETAGNE

Ginsterlicht, gelb, die Hänge
eitern gen Himmel, der Dorn
wirbt um die Wunde, es läutet
darin, es ist Abend, das Nichts
rollt seine Meere zur Andacht,
das Blutsegel hält auf dich zu.

Trocken, verlandet
das Bett hinter dir, verschilft
seine Stunde, oben,
beim Stern, die milchigen
Priele schwatzen im Schlamm, Steindattel,
unten, gebuscht, klafft ins Gebläu, eine Staude
Vergänglichkeit, schön,
grüßt dein Gedächtnis.

(Kanntet ihr mich,
Hände? Ich ging
den gegabelten Weg, den ihr wiest, mein Mund
spie seinen Schotter, ich ging, meine Zeit,
wandernde Wächte, warf ihren Schatten—kanntet ihr mich?)

Hände, die dorn-
umworbene Wunde, es läutet,
Hände, das Nichts, seine Meere,
Hände, im Ginsterlicht, das
Blutsegel
hält auf dich zu.

Du
du lehrst
du lehrst deine Hände
du lehrst deine Hände du lehrst

[2] Celan (1983), 1:171.

4

du lehrst deine Hände
>schlafen

[MATIÈRE DE BRETAGNE

Gorselight, yellow, the slopes
suppurate to heaven, the thorn
pays court to the wound, there is ringing
inside, it is evening, the nothing
rolls its seas toward devotion,
the bloodsail is heading for you.

Dry, run aground
is the bed behind you, caught in rushes
is its hour, above,
with the star, the milky
tideways jabber in mud, stonedate,
below, bunched up, gapes into blueness, a bush-worth
of transience, beautiful,
greets your memory.

(Did you know me,
hands? I went
the forked way you showed, my mouth
spat its gravel, I went, my time,
wandering watches, threw its shadow—did you know me?)

Hands, the thorn-
courted wound, there is ringing,
hands, the nothing, its seas,
hands, in the gorselight, the
bloodsail
is heading for you.

You
you teach
you teach your hands
you teach your hands you teach
you teach your hands
>to sleep]

What is "gorselight"? Yellow broom flowers. To another poet they might be beautiful, for Celan they suppurate. Their phrasing recalls the first verse of Hölderlin's poem "Hälfte des Lebens" ("Half of Life"): compare the sound of *Ginsterlicht, gelb, die Hänge* and *Mit gelben Birnen hänget*.[3] But whereas Hölderlin's yellow pears are steeped in beauty, Celan's gorse issues pus. The contrast suggests a mood. The mood continues quietly in Celan's imagery of thorn and wound, as Christian and courtly conventions of love combine toward "devotion" (*Andacht*). But what sails toward devotion is "the Nothing" (*das Nichts*) and the mood swerves into negative theology. As any reader of Celan knows, he is at home in this mood. Here, however, it may be meant to evoke that other "poet of nothingness" whose verse is full of seas and sailing, Mallarmé.[4] Remember the tenth double-page of *Un Coup de dés,* which begins with the word *RIEN* high on the left-hand side and is typeset so that the rest of the words roll themselves out across the page in waves to end in "the wave in which all reality dissolves" at the lower right.[5] Finally, Celan's sea is also a sea of romance bringing Isolt to Tristan on a ship that flies a "bloodsail."

All these fluent traditions run aground in the second stanza, which is dry, stuck on land, lodged in rushes, bushed up, jabbering mud and which engenders the third stanza: five verses stalled in a bracket. The poet's thought stops on itself. His path is forked and his utterance gravel. Celan has crafted these middle verses out of immobility to emphasize the movement of the rest. Seas and phenomena flow again in the fourth stanza and go rolling out the end of the page without a stop. The poem as a whole, recapitulating the first stanza, has the rhythm of a bloodsail, sailing forward in waves from gorselight to gorselight to you.

[3] This connection was suggested by Stanley Corngold, whose conversation with me about Celan's poem made this essay possible.

[4] The label is Sartre's, who also cites George Poulet: "From the outset Mallarmé's poetry is like a mirage . . . in which he recognized himself not by where or how he is but by where he is not and how he is not." Sartre (1988), 112.

[5] Mallarmé (1977), 290–191. There are not a few echoes of Mallarmé throughout the poem, especially in the ringing (cf. Mallarmé's "Le Sonneur") and the blueness (cf. "L'Azur"), not to say the arranged white space into which all disappears at the end.

Celan's "you" is hard to fix, as his bloodsail is a difficult color. If he means a reference to the Tristan legend, the sail should be either white or black. Tristan had arranged this signal with the helmsman bringing Isolt to him by sea: a white sail for Isolt prospering, a black sail for her catastrophe. When Tristan's jealous wife reports to him that the sail is "blacker than a mulberry," Tristan turns his face to the wall and dies.[6] There is blood in the old French version but only dreamblood; as Tristan lies dying, Isolt out at sea recalls dreaming that she held in her lap the head of a boar that was staining her all over with its blood and making her robe red.

Blood of course might signify simply fatality. Sail that kills. But let us consider the matter historically. Our oldest literary example of the trope of the false sail comes from the ancient Greek poet Simonides (556–467 B.C.). Simonides mentions the sail and calls it red: φοινίκεον. Indeed he mentions it *in order to call it red*, in defiance of an existing tradition. For the false sail was already an old story by Simonides' time, part of the myth of Theseus, of which other versions existed. Simonides did not scruple to waste a few more words on the subject. The poem he composed is not extant, but we do have two fragmentary citations. From Plutarch we get news of the sail:

> Then Theseus cheered his father by boasting that he would defeat the Minotaur. So his father gave the helmsman a second sail, white this time, telling him to hoist the white sail if he were returning with Theseus safe, otherwise to sail with the black and so signify catastrophe. But Simonides says that the sail given by Aigeus was "not white but a red sail (φοινίκεον ἱστίον) dyed with the wet flower of the blooming holm-oak" and that this was to be the sign of their salvation.[7]

And from a scholiast we have the words of the messenger sent by Theseus to his father on the day of his return. For according to

---

[6] Does the wife lie or is the ship flying the wrong sail? Throughout the old French *version commune* (which, I assume from the title of his poem, is the one Celan has in mind), this point remains unresolved. Spector (1973), 85.

[7] Plutarch *Life of Theseus* 17.4; Simonides fr. 550 *PMG*.

legend, Theseus is sailing into harbor when he realizes that he forgot to hoist the white sail. A messenger is dispatched to bring the true story to the father, but Aigeus has already read the death-sail and accepted its version. He throws himself into the sea. The messenger is addressing the father's corpse when he says:

βιότου κέ σε μᾶλλον ὄνασα πρότερος ἐλθών.

[I would have given you a profit greater than life if I had come sooner.][8]

Simonides' messenger states his case as economically as possible. His verb (ὄνασα, from ὀνίνημι "to profit") is drawn from the sphere of commercial gain. More important, his statement takes the form of a contrary-to-fact condition. Why must the economy of the false sail be contrafactual? Because it is an impossible idea conditioned by the negative event that already exists. Two realities for the price of one. No profit in fact changes hands—but the idea of it, added to the account contrafactually, multiplies pathos and learning. Aigeus' salvation is both adduced and canceled in the messenger's spare comment. You could have your sail and falsify it too, if words were true.

White, black, red, telling, lying, lied about, forgotten, fatal, all in all the falsity of the false sail is a rich proposition. How such propositions extend themselves to form the interior of a poem like "Matière de Bretagne" is hard to say. Celan combines the local Bretagne stuff of courtly traditions and ancient sailing with the local Bretagne stuff of gravel, hours, beds and personal pronouns that fold over one another like hands. He transcribes a circle of great lyrical beauty, lit by gorselight, around Nothing-ness. *Das Nichts* occurs twice but this word does not stop the poem or spoil the light. It is simply part of the poet's *matière*. So too Simonides constructs the truth about the false sail negatively. "Not white but red," he insists and then goes on to matters of local color: "dyed with the wet flower of the blooming holm-oak." The redness of his red sail stains fact deeply with the fixative of coun-

8 Scholiast *ad* Sophokles *Ajax* 740; Simonides fr. 551 *PMG*.

terfact. Redder than red, redder than the blood of a boar in a dream, is the φοινίκεον that rests on white nothing.

Negation links the mentalities of Simonides and Celan. Words for "no," "not," "never," "nowhere," "nobody," "nothing" dominate their poems and create bottomless places for reading. Not white but red. Was it not Aristotle who said, "A mistake enriches the mere truth once you see it as that." Both Simonides and Celan are poets who see it as that. And ask us to see it as that. Us in the gorselight.

That is why the whole of Celan's poem gathers us into a movement—toward you—that sails to the end. But you, by the time we reach you, are just folding yourself away into a place we cannot go: sleep. Blank spaces instead of words fill out the verses around you as if to suggest your gradual recession down and away from our grasp. What could your hands teach us if you had not vanished? To stand at this border with whiteness exhausts our power of listening and makes us aware of a crisis in you. We travel toward your crisis, we arrive, yet we cannot construe it—the terrible thing is, after all (and most economically!) we are the false sail for which you wait.

CHAPTER I

Alienation

SIMONIDES

Simonides of Keos was the smartest person in the fifth century
B.C., or so I have come to believe. History has it that he was also
the stingiest. Fantastical in its anecdotes, undeniable in its impli-
cations, the stinginess of Simonides can tell us something about
the moral life of a user of money and something about the poetic
life of an economy of loss.

No one who uses money is unchanged by that.

No one who uses money can easily get a look at their own prac-
tice. *Ask eye to see its own eyelashes,* as the Chinese proverb says. Yet
Simonides did so, not only because he was smart. History placed
Simonides on the cusp of two economic systems. His life forms a
kind of pointed projection arising at the place where coined
money transected the premonetary culture of archaic Greece.

COIN

A coin is a flattened piece of metal of standardized weight with a
design imprinted on one or both sides to indicate what individual
or community issued it and will receive it again. The first true
coinage, Herodotos tell us, was a Lydian invention and so datable
to about 700 B.C.[1] Lydian coins were originally of electrum, a nat-
ural alloy of gold and silver. On the Greek mainland the cities of
Corinth and Athens began to strike coins of silver before 550 and
by the end of the sixth century the use of coinage was widespread
throughout the Greek world.

[1] Herodotos 1.94.

10

But the monetary system of the Greek world was anarchic in early times. Each city could enforce the circulation of its own currency internally but abroad coins were accepted only on the basis of weight. Moreover, their large denominations suggest that the earliest coins were struck not for commercial use in local markets but to facilitate government bureaucracy (e.g., for paying mercenaries, financing public works and cults, discharging harbor tolls or other taxes).[2] Private individuals surely found uses for currency, which increasingly came to dominate retail trade and personal order, but money did not simply *replace* the premonetary structures of economic life. Rather, it penetrated these gradually and unevenly over the course of several centuries, meanwhile enjoying a weird coexistence with anachronistic systems of exchange whose activity in fact contradicted the monetary rationale in important particulars.[3]

GIFT

Before there is money, many complex societies order their economic lives, to a significant extent,[4] by means of gifts and gift exchange. Historians have shown how an ideology of aristocratic gift exchange, conspicuous throughout the Homeric poems and also well evidenced in archaeological remains of the Homeric world, continued to inform the archaic and classical Greek societies of the eighth to the fourth centuries B.C., coexisting tenaciously with the spread of money and commodity exchange.[5] Gift

[2] Kraay (1964); Starr (1977), 112–18; Kroll and Waggoner (1984).

[3] "It is probably best to view early Greek coinage as the incorporation of a novel form of wealth into pre-existing channels of exchange and as a symbol of political independence, rather than as an indication of the appearance of the pre-requisites of wage labor." Morris (1986), 6. See also Kurke (1995).

[4] Piracy, pillage, barter and trade may operate alongside gift exchange: the complex cooperation of these systems in premarket societies is analyzed (generally) by Polanyi (1957); and Sahlins (1972); (specifically for Greeks) by Finley (1935, 1953); Gregory (1982); Polanyi (1968); and Starr (1977).

[5] Gregory (1982), 48–50; Kurke (1991), 93–97; (1995); Morris (1986), 8–9; Starr (1970), 58–60; Turner (1974), 14.

exchange forms part of what is called an "embedded economy," that is, a sociocultural system in which the elements of economic life are embedded in noneconomic institutions like kinship, marriage, hospitality, artistic patronage and ritual friendship. These function through a maze of social, religious and symbolic interactions whose core is the exchange of gifts.[6]

Marcel Mauss initiated the study of gifts and gift economy in his celebrated *Essai sur le don*. Here he describes societies where gift-giving is a mechanism of exchange that is at once material and moral and knits the community together in a living fabric of value. Mauss cites a proverb from New Caledonia:

> Our feasts are the movement of a needle which sews together the parts of our reed roofs, making of these a single roof, one word.[7]

Mauss emphasizes that such a "single roof" is continuously woven out of three interrelated obligations: to give, to receive, to repay. Considering these three requirements, we begin to see how the moral life established by such transactions differs from that of a money economy. A gift has both economic and spiritual content, is personal and reciprocal, and depends on a relationship that endures over time. Money is an abstraction that passes one way and impersonally between people whose relationship stops with the transfer of cash. To use Marx's terms, a commodity is an alienable object exchanged between two transactors enjoying a state of mutual independence, while a gift is an inalienable object exchanged between two reciprocally dependent transactors.[8] Gift and commodity represent two different notions of value, embodied in two different sets of social relations. The sets ought to be mutually exclusive. In fact, historically and psychologically, they overlap.

---

[6] Austin and Vidal-Naquet (1977), 12, 177–78; Bourdieu (1977), 171; Kurke (1991), 85–107; Polanyi (1968), 81–82.

[7] Mauss (1967), 9.

[8] Marx (1867), 1:178; Morris (1986), 2.

XENIA

Take for example the mode of gift exchange that the ancient Greeks call ξενία (*xenia*). Usually translated "hospitality" or "guest-friendship" or "ritualized friendship," the institution of *xenia* pervades the socioeconomic interactions of the Homeric, archaic and classical periods. Gabriel Herman defines *xenia* as "a bond of solidarity manifesting itself in an exchange of goods and services between individuals originating from separate social units."[9] The characteristic features of *xenia*, namely its basis in reciprocation and its assumption of perpetuity, seem to have woven a texture of personal alliances that held the ancient world together.

In spirit, *xenia* is emphatically nonmercantile: goods are not measured, profit is not the point.[10] In fact, the point is to put yourself in debt:

> The aim of the gift economy is accumulation for de-accumulation; the gift economy is above all a debt economy, where the actors strive to maximize outgoings. The system can be described as one of "alternating disequilibrium" where the aim is never to have debts "paid off" but to preserve a situation of personal indebtedness. [11]

For whereas money is concerned to change the status quo, gifts aim to sustain it. The profound conservatism of a gift economy secures its own continuance and moral prestige in two ways. First, by derogation of all that is not gift. We can see a deep mistrust of money, trade, profit, commerce and commercial persons pervading Greek socioeconomic attitudes from Homer's time through Aristotle's. "Commodity exchange was not an acceptable activity

[9] Herman (1987), 10.

[10] But see Sahlins (1972), 298ff. on the weighing of gifts; Starr (1977), 58–60 on economic motives in exchange; Herman (1987), 61 on the questions raised by "Glaukos who exchanged with Diomedes armor of gold for armor of bronze" (*Iliad* 6.234–36).

[11] Morris (1986), 2; Herman (1987), 10.

for a Greek," one historian concludes.[12] Wealth is a good thing to have but not a good thing to *go after*. At the same time, a gift economy likes to project its functions onto the cosmos, Mauss suggests, as if the rules of *xenia* represent simply *the way things are* for gods and men. Gift exchange endures by misrecognition of the fact that it is just one economic system among others.[13] Solon, a politician who lived in a period of flourishing commerce and founded a career on the denunciation of money, speaks as a typical sixth-century aristocrat when he says:

> Perfectly happy is the man who has lovely boys and horses with
>   solid hooves
> and hunting dogs and a *xenos* in foreign places.[14]

Delicate Situation of the Ancient Poet

Poets from ancient times participated in the gift economy of their communities as *xenoi* of the people who enjoyed their poetry. Homer shows us Demodokos and Phemios as permanent court singers who traded their songs for the hospitality of the house and Odysseus himself making ad hoc exchange of his story for food and shelter. At the moment when Odysseus, in the banquet hall of Alkinoos, carves out a hot chunk of pig meat from his own portion and proffers it in gratitude to the singer Demodokos "so that he may eat and so that I may fold him close to me," we see the embedded economy in its ideal version.[15] During the centuries that followed, poets like Stesichoros, Xenophanes, Ibykos, Anakreon, Simonides, Aiskhylos, Pindar and Bakkhylides traveled to

---

[12] Morris (1986), 5–6. See also Blank (1985) on Platonic and other disapproval of sophists for charging fees; Kerferd (1981), 26–28 on sophists; Connor (1971), 171–73 on the huckstering of demagogues; Nestle (1942), 455–76 on the treatment of these issues in Old Comedy.

[13] Mauss (1967), 13; Bourdieu (1977), 171–77; Kurke (1991), 96; (1995).

[14] Solon fr. 13 West.

[15] Homer *Odyssey* 8.87–103; 9.1–13; 8.477–78. On the ancient poet's situation, see especially Svenbro (1976).

the cities of their patrons and lived in their houses while producing poetry for them. Describing such a relationship between Polykrates the tyrant and the poet Anakreon, Strabo says, "Anakreon the lyric poet lived with this man and all his poetry is full of his memory." Herodotos gives a picture of Polykrates and Anakreon "conversing as they recline side by side in the dining hall."[16] We recognize the external structure of the relationship as one of aristocratic *xenia,* with gifts of poetry exchanged for gifts of livelihood by men who know a mutual and ritual connection. We can only imagine its delicate internal workings.

Money changed all this. "Money," says Marx, "is the externalization of all the capacities of humanity."[17]

CHANGE

Simonides was held responsible for the change. According to an ancient scholiast, "Simonides was the first poet who introduced meticulous calculation into songmaking and composed poems for a price."[18] From this fact depends an elaborate iconology that represents Simonides as a miser, curmudgeon and sordid money-grubber. "No one would deny that Simonides loved money," is the bald assertion of his biographer Ailian. His contemporary, the poet Xenophanes, labels Simonides *kimbix* (κίμβιξ: "skinflint"). Within fifty years of his death Simonides appears as a stock type of avarice on the comic stage. One Aristophanic character comments, "That Simonides would put out to sea on a bathmat for profit!" Aristotle uses Simonides in much the same way, as a stock ethical exemplum of *aneleutheria* (ἀνελευθερία: "miserliness").[19]

[16] Strabo 14.638; Herodotos 3.121.

[17] McLellan (1977), 111.

[18] Kallimachos fr. 222 Pfeiffer; Suidas *s.v.* Simonides; Bell (1978); Fränkel (1973), 493; Gzella (1971); Kurke (1991), 7.

[19] Ailian 9.1; Xenophanes, whose comment is preserved by the scholiast on Aristophanes *Peace* 697, may have met Simonides at the court of Hieron in Syracuse (see Bell [1978], 34; Gzella [1971]); Aristophanes *Peace* 695; Aristotle *Nicomachean Ethics* 1121a6–7; cf. *Rhetoric* 1391a8ff.

Other testimonia record that Simonides demanded enormous fees for his verse, hoarded money in jars in his house, journeyed around the world in search of rich patrons, denounced those who did not pay him enough and delivered homilies on the pleasures of profit. It would be plausible enough, especially in light of the characterological tendency of ancient biographers,[20] to dismiss these stories as a biographical trope for the simple fact of Simonides' professionalization of poetry. But let us try to understand the simple fact more precisely.

That Simonides was the first to professionalize poetry is not unlikely. Somebody had to do it and current beliefs about the date of the circulation of coinage coincide with his lifetime.[21]

That Simonides made lots of money is not impossible. We have some information about wages in the early fifth century that indicates the verbal arts were comparatively well paid. For example, Phidias the sculptor worked on the chryselephantine statue of Athena in Athens for 5,000 drachmas per year, out of which he had to pay himself, his workmen and his production costs.[22] And Herodotos tells us of a successful doctor whose annual salary was 6,000 drachmas when he lived in Aegina, 12,000 drachmas when he lived on Samos, 10,000 drachmas when he lived in Athens. This same amount, 10,000 drachmas, was the fee commanded by Pindar for a single dithyramb composed in honor of the Athenians. Meanwhile Gorgias the sophist required his students to pay him 10,000 drachmas apiece for a single course in rhetoric and made enough money this way to erect a solid gold statue of himself in the precinct of Apollo at Delphi. Sokrates asserts that both Gorgias and Prodikos "earned more from his wisdom than any other craftsman from his art."[23] It has been estimated that 10,000

[20] On ancient styles in biography, see Bell (1978); Dihle (1956); Momigliano (1971), 68–73.

[21] Figueira (1981), 80–97, 108; Kraay (1976), 13–27; Kroll and Waggoner (1984); Kurke (1995), 39 n.12.

[22] Donnay (1967); Gentili (1988), 162.

[23] Herodotos 3.131; scholiast *ad* Pindar *Nemeans* 5; [Plato] *Hippias major* 282c–d.

drachmas would have been equivalent to about twenty-eight years of work for a laborer at one drachma *per diem*.[24]

That Simonides devoted his life to avarice is hard to prove or disprove since, despite centuries of unanimous testimonial ranting about Simonidean greed, no source preserves a single account or real number to tell us how avid he was, how rich he became or what prices he actually charged. Evidently Simonidean greed was more resented in its essence than in its particulars. Its essence was the commodification of a previously reciprocal and ritual activity, the exchange of gifts between friends.

OBJECT

Commodification marks a radical moment in the history of human culture. People who use money seem to form different relationships with one another and with objects than people who do not. Marx gave the name "alienation" to this difference.[25] Marx believed that money makes the objects we use into alien things and makes the people with whom we exchange them into alien people. "Money is the pimp between man's need and the object, between his life and his means of life. But that which mediates my life for me also mediates the existence of other people for me. Money becomes the *Other*."[26] When Marx describes the complex process by which commodification changes people, he is talking about bourgeois society and modern capitalist economies, not about the fifth century B.C. But the terms of his description may help us see Simonides' situation more clearly. For Marx is also,

[24] Diogenes Laertios 9.52; Pliny *Natural History* 33.24 (cf. Athenaios 505d); see also Plato *Protagoras* 328b; Suidas s.v. *Gorgias;* Kerferd (1981) 25; Blank (1985), 5. Plato the comic poet mentions the φιλαργυρία of sophists (fr. 103 Kock); Athenaios records that Gorgias attributed his long life to his "never having done anything free for the sake of another" (548c–d).

[25] "Alienation" is the English word usually chosen to translate two terms, *Entfremdung* and *Entäusserung*, that Marx used indiscriminately or sometimes together: McLellan (1977), 110.

[26] Struik (1964), 75.

always, talking about the most fundamental ethics of exchange and its objects.

Let us take a moment to consider the life of objects. Within a gift economy, as we have seen, objects in exchange form a kind of connective tissue between giver and receiver. The reciprocal character of the connection is implied in its reversible terminology: in Greek the word *xenos* can mean either guest or host, *xenia* either gifts given or gifts received. "Considered as an act of communication," says Pierre Bourdieu, "the gift is defined by the counter-gift in which it is completed and in which it realizes its full significance."[27] Such an object carries the history of the giver into the life of the receiver and continues it there. Because they valued this continuity, the Greeks created a remarkably concrete token of it that was used as a sign of mutual obligation between friends, the object called a *symbolon* (σύμβολον):

> People who entered into relationships of *xenia* used to cut a piece of bone in two and keep one half themselves and leave the other with their partners, so that if they or their friends or relatives should have occasion to visit them or *vice versa,* they might bring the half with them and renew the *xenia.*[28]

Symbola were not a standard feature of every *xenia* relationship but their concept is suggestive of the nonobjective life of objects in these exchanges. A gift is not a piece broken off from the interior life of the giver and lost into the exchange, but rather an extension of the interior of the giver, both in space and in time, into the interior of the receiver. Money denies such extension, ruptures continuity and stalls objects at the borders of themselves. Abstracted from space and time as bits of saleable value, they become commodities and lose their life as objects.

For a commodity is not an object, it is a quantity of value that can be measured against or substituted for other such quantities. In commodification its natural properties are extinguished. Extinguished also is its power to connect the people who give and receive

---

[27] Bourdieu in Peristiany (1966), 210.
[28] Scholiast *ad* Euripides *Helen* 291; Herman (1987), 63. See also Gauthier (1972).

it: they become like commodities themselves, fragments of value waiting for price and sale. They take on "commodity form."[29]

GRACE AND HARE

Commodity form is not a simple state of mind. It fragments and dehumanizes human being. It causes a person to assume a "double character" wherein his natural properties are disjunct from his economic value, his private from his public self.[30] These are the terms in which Marx described the effect of commodification on citizens of bourgeois Europe. I like to think Simonides represents an early, severe form of economic alienation and the "doubleness" that attends it. Finding himself born into a society where traditions of gift exchange coexisted with commodity trade and a flourishing money economy, balanced on a borderline between two economic systems and inserted into the disintegrating consciousness of that time, he took a naked view. He uncovered his eyes in both directions.

Plato tells us how it was that Simonides came to Athens:

> Hipparchos, eldest and wisest of the sons of Peisistratos, arranged to have Simonides of Keos in continual attendance upon him by the inducement of *big wages and gifts*.[31]

Wages and gifts: the coin has two sides. Reality being twofold, Simonides insisted on pointing to both sides of it. Hence, for example, the story of his two boxes of grace.

> They say that Simonides had two boxes, one for graces, the other for fees. So when someone came to him asking for a grace he had the boxes displayed and opened: the one was found to be empty of graces, the other full of money. And that's the way Simonides got rid of a person requesting a gift.[32]

---

[29] On commodity and commodity form, see Marx (1973), 78 and (1967), 141; Löwith (1993), 89–102; McLellan (1977), 295; Pilling (1980), 145.

[30] Löwith (1993), 93–95.

[31] [Plato] *Hippias Major* 228c (my emphasis).

[32] Scholiast *ad* Theokritos 16; Stobaios 10.39; Aristophanes *Peace* 697; Plutarch *Moralia* 520a, 555–56; Bell (1978); MacLachlan (1993).

The two boxes stand side by side in Simonides' life as gifts and money coexist in his society. Their alignment sets up an economic thought-experiment. For the Greek word χάρις (*charis:* "grace") that names the emptiness of the first box was a key term in the gift-exchange economy of the archaic and classical periods, designating "a willing and precious reciprocal exchange" between men who knew a mutual and ritual dependence.[33] Like *xenos* and *xenia,* the word *charis* is semantically reversible and includes in its lexical equivalents favor, gift, goodwill given or received, payment, repayment, gratification, pleasure afforded or pleasure returned, charity, grace, Grace. In other words, *charis* is the generic name for the whole texture of exchanges that constitutes a gift economy as well as for the piety that guarantees them. So Aristotle inserts into his analysis of money in the *Nicomachean Ethics* a rather wistful passing salute to the goddesses called the *Charites:*

> That is why people build a temple to the *Charites* in a conspicuous place, so that there may be reciprocal giving. For this is the essence of *charis:* the necessity both to repay a grace done to oneself and also to initiate gracious action on one's own.[34]

The idea of containing this living texture of actions, emotions, value, tradition and time in a box is more than cynical, it is surreal. The proposal to dip into this box and pull out a bit of grace to give to a total stranger belies the entire social and historical rationale of the word *charis,* its reciprocal and continuative essence. The notion that grace can live in a box is just about as crazy as the notion that little pieces of metal are equivalent to everything in the world, including a poem of Simonides. And yet, the reality is—there stands the other box: hard, cold shape of the future, full of cash. "Money can exchange any quality or object for any other, even contradictory qualities and objects," says Marx.

> It is the fraternization of incompatibles, it forces contraries to embrace. If you suppose man to be man and his relation to be a human

---

[33] Kurke (1991), 67; further on *charis,* see Compagner (1988), 77–93; Hands (1968), 20–38; Herman (1987), 41–48, 129; Hewitt (1927), 142–61; Humphreys (1978), 31–75; Löw (1908); MacLachlan (1993); Morris (1986), 1–17.

[34] Aristotle *Nicomachean Ethics* 1133a2–6.

one, then you can only exchange love for love, trust for trust, etc. . . . But money is the enemy of man and social bonds. It changes fidelity into infidelity, love into hate, hate into love, virtue into vice, vice into virtue, slave into master, master into slave, stupidity into wisdom, wisdom into stupidity. It is the universal confusion and exchange of all things, an inverted world.[35]

Simonides is like someone trying to live upright in an inverted world. Various anecdotes of his traditional biography picture him off balance with his hosts or patrons, groping for the grace of the relationship. He visits these people's houses and sits at their tables, but the hospitality they offer him is oddly qualified. Take the matter of hare:

> Chamailion (speaking of hares) says that one day Simonides was feasting wth Hieron when hare was served to the other guests. But none to Simonides. Later Hieron gave him a portion and he improvised this verse: "Wide it was but not wide enough to reach this far."[36]

Simonides' improvisation is a parody of a verse in Homer: "Wide it was but not a wide enough shore to contain all the ships."[37] Likening skimpy hare to the beach at Troy is a witticism aimed at easing an awkward social moment. But it may also cast a wry side glance at an earlier age and other values. Homer's community would surely have guaranteed him not only a complete dinner but a full livelihood, "so that he might eat and so that he might be folded close," as Odysseus once said.[38] In his study of ritual friendship, Herman emphasizes that *xenia* is a relationship between people who feel responsible for one another's well-being in "a range of cooperative acts as wide as one could possibly find in any human society. . . . The reason for this was that ritualised friendship acted both as a substitute for and above all a complement to kinship roles." And therefore the transactions of *xenia* ought not to be mixed with those of commodity trade, which places different boundaries around the act of exchange. "Transactions of ritu-

---

[35] McLellan (1977), 111.
[36] Simonides fr. 7 West; Athenaios 656c.
[37] *Iliad* 14.33; cf. Eustathios 1821.37.
[38] *Odyssey* 8.477–78 and above.

alised friendship were supposed to be carried out in a non-mercantile spirit," Herman maintains. "Excluded are relations between strangers that involve payments for goods and services. . . . People trading specific goods and services for payments would hardly classify their relationship as one of friendship."[39]

Yet what if they did?

Herman does not mention the delicate situation of the ancient poet, who is both *xenos* and employee, both friend and hireling, of his patron. Let us imagine Simonides, who has received cash payment from Hieron for a commissioned poem earlier in the day, seated beside the tyrant at dinner. What more does Hieron owe him? What are the rules for this? Money has quantified the moral tension between them and liquidated their mutual responsibility. Money has filled the box of grace with Syrakusan coin. Money has imploded the meaning of *xenos*. For alongside "guest" and "host," the Greek word *xenos* denotes "stranger," "outsider," "alien." At one time it made sense to blend these meanings in a single word because the reality was unitary. Stranded between "guest" and "alien," Simonides sits watching this rich and ancient reality fall apart like an overcooked hare.

SNOW

Simonides got short-changed on snow too. Athenaios tells the story of how Simonides once "was feasting with some people in a season of terrific heat. The wine waiters were mixing snow into the drinks of everybody else but not into his." So he improvised this poem:

> τήν ῥά ποτ᾽ Οὐλύμποιο περὶ πλευρὰς ἐκάλυψεν
>   ὠκὺς ἀπὸ Θρήικης ὀρνύμενος Βορέης,
> ἀνδρῶν δ᾽ ἀχλαίνων ἔδακεν φρένας, αὐτὰρ ἐκάμφθη
>   ζωὴ Πιερίην γῆν ἐπιεσσαμένη,
> ἔν τις ἐμοὶ καὶ τῆς χείτω μέρος· οὐ γὰρ ἔοικεν
>   θερμὴν βαστάζειν ἀνδρὶ φίλωι πρόποσιν.[40]

---

[39] Herman (1987), 128, 10.
[40] Simonides fr. 88 *FGE;* 6 West; Athenaios 125c–d.

[The stuff that quick Boreas shooting out of Thrace once
    wrapped around the ribs of Olympos,
and it bit the lungs of cloakless men, but was curved
    as a living garment about the Pierian land—
let someone pour some of that into my drink. For it
    is not seemly to lift a hot pledge to a man beloved.]

The poem begins slow and cold as if it were setting up a riddle, then flashes into hot rebuke. Verses 1–4 have the standard form of a riddle, three frigidly phrased clues whose referent is "snow." The riddle (*griphos*) was a popular form of after-dinner entertainment and Athenaios tells us Simonides was an expert riddler. He preserves two examples of Simonidean riddles (both incomprehensible to me) and appends a list of popularly conjectured solutions: "Some people explain the riddle thus . . . but others say . . . and others again. . . ."[41] The point is, good riddles do not say what they mean. It is an innately stingy form of discourse, disguising its data and begrudging its truth. "You know the riddle advertises all the tecnhiques that the joke conceals," said Freud.[42] The riddle advertises everything except its own punchline. Odd, then, that Simonides drops the riddle form in the last two verses of his poem and gives his punchline away. This is no idle generosity. These verses are framed in the diction of social decorum ("it is not seemly" . . . "a man beloved") to remind his host that certain rules of grace are in abeyance at this dinner table. Where love is the structure of hospitality, neither host nor guest withholds what is seemly from the other. But money changes the relations between people, makes a riddle out of human *philia*.

Simonides' poem transcends its riddling purpose and graceless occasion. There is an archness in the way the poet phrases his appeal for snow in terms of reciprocity: after all, the snow is not for his own pleasure but to raise a pledge to his host! There is a realism in the way he balances this bravado against tender allusion to the poet's dependent situation: imagery of blasting winter wind and men exposed. This may be a quiet instance of that topos

[41] Athenaios 456c.
[42] Letter to Sandor Ferenczi: Gay (1988), 188.

we find in Greek poetry, of the shivering needy poet who receives a cloak in recompense for lyric service.[43] At any rate, when we read in Stobaios how Simonides, questioned about his love of money, answered:

> I would rather bequeath it to enemies after I am dead than beg it from friends while I am alive![44]

we appreciate his reasoning. The answer is a bleak play upon those archaic values of love and hate, friend and enemy, which would in more graceful times have liberated the poet from economic questions altogether.

ONE IS AN EATER

You cannot eat money. You can, on the other hand, sell food. In fact you can sell anything. Marx called this fact "commodity form" and believed it to characterize the life of all objects in a money economy. "Selling is the practice of alienation," he says, "and the commodity is its expression."[45] So expressed, commodities acquire a value estranged from their use and abstracted from their context of use. Simonides experienced this loss of context from the inside. In his relations with the patrons who were also his hosts, he saw decorum break down. He watched great rents and tears beginning to appear in the the texture of reciprocal action that was supposed to contain and nurture a poet's life. He watched *xenia* being measured out to him as a commodity. He became sharply aware of his own exchange value as a producer of poetry. And with the dry clarity that characterized his social genius, he transferred these inconcinnities to action:

> Simonides really was a sordid greedy skinflint, you know: in Syrakuse (as Chamailion tells it) Hieron was in the habit of dispatching to the poet a daily portion of food. Simonides brightly sold the greater part

---

[43] E.g., Hipponax fr. 32 and 34 West; Aristophanes *Birds* 904ff.
[44] Stobaios 3.79.
[45] Marx, "On the Jewish Question," in Bottomore (1963), 39.

of it, keeping just a small share for himself. And when someone asked "Why?" he answered: *"So that Hieron's munificence* (μεγαλοπρέπεια) *may be obvious to all, not to mention my own sense of order* (κοσμιότης)."[46]

Once again Simonides is pointing to a tension between two economic systems. Food is transformed into money in the story, as use value is transformed into exchange value when a society adopts coinage. This transformation has less to do with personal avarice than with the reduction of all human values to commensurability. Simonides' wording is deliberate. *Megaloprepeia* ("munificence") and *kosmiotēs* ("sense of order") are terms drawn directly from the aristocratic vocabulary of gift exchange.[47] They sort incongruously with the act of commodity exchange in which the poet is engaged. But the incongruity starts with Hieron. Why is he sending Simonides a take-out dinner instead of folding him close in traditional commensality? Money changes relations between people, it comes in-between their hands. Money disembeds the graceful gestures of an aristocratic economy and inscribes them on the surfaces of artifact. The tradition of Simonidean avarice represents a powerful abstraction of that reality, measuring the gap that was beginning to open up between poet and patron in this new age of commerce and professionalism. The fifth-century poet is no longer a member of the same social body as his audience. Nor do the operations of *xenia* suffice to assimilate him. Like food sold for money, the professional poet remains unincorporably alien.

Now it is true in ancient Greek as in many other cultures that difference defines the poet. Homer would not be blind if the truth were generally apparent. Simonides would not be a miser unless language were one of the most telling economies we use. But there is a deep crack that runs between the blindness of Homer and the avarice of Simonides. The society that revered Homer's insight has become, by the fifth century, an audience suspicious of Simonides' economic expertise. We have seen in the poems and anecdotes above that Simonides likes to play upon his

[46] Athenaios 14.656d (my emphasis).

[47] Μεγαλοπρέπεια: Aristotle *Nicomachean Ethics* 1123a; Kurke (1991, 171–94; κοσμιότης: Plato *Gorgias* 508a; Aristotle *Nicomachean Ethics* 1109a.

own alienation. Underlying this play is (I think) serious thought about the meaning of poetic vocation.

Selling poems provokes thought about what their value is and who can measure that. We know Simonides entertained these questions and that he dealt sharply with anyone who presumed to answer them for him. Aristotle recounts, for example, the story of a victor in the mule race who wished to buy from Simonides a victory ode. Simonides declined, because the fee was small and he didn't like the idea of writing poetry for mules.

> But on being given adequate payment, he made this verse:
>
> Hail you daughters of storm-footed horses![48]

Adequate pay calls forth an adequate poem. Let us balance this anecdote against another from the biographical tradition, concerned with the opposite end of the payment scale. One day, so the story goes, Simonides, on the eve of departure for an oceanic journey, was walking by himself along the seashore. Suddenly he stopped. There was a corpse at his feet. Simonides did not delay. He set about burying the corpse and then erected an epitaph. It speaks in the voice of the dead man:

οἱ μὲν ἐμὲ κτείναντες ὁμοίων ἀντιτύχοιεν,
   Ζεῦ ξένι', οἱ δ' ὑπὸ γᾶν θέντες ὄναιντο βίου.[49]

[I pray those who killed me get the same themselves,
   O Zeus of guest and host,
I pray those who put me in the ground
   enjoy the profit of life.]

But the epitaph is not the end of the story. During the night, the corpse that Simonides had buried appeared to him in a dream and advised him not to set sail the next day. Simonides communicated this warning to his fellow-travelers, who disregarded it, set sail and were shipwrecked. Simonides stayed behind alone and was saved. He then erected a codicil to the epitaph on the beach:

---

[48] Aristotle *Rhetoric* 1405b = Simonides fr. 515 *PMG*.
[49] Simonides fr. 84 *FGE; Palatine Anthology* 7.516.

οὗτος ὁ τοῦ Κείοιο Σιμωνίδου ἐστὶ σαωτήρ,
ὃς καὶ τεθνηὼς ζῶντι παρέσχε χάριν.[50]

[This is Simonides' savior
  who even though dead has bestowed on the living a grace.]

Characteristically, Simonides makes a double statement about the economics of his situation. For he addresses the epitaph proper to Zeus Xenios, "God of guest and host," whose primordial rules of hospitality to strangers will have dictated the poet's burial of the corpse found on a beach. At the same time he frames the dead man's prayer of revenge in language of profit and loss, just a tinge of market mentality to underline the absence of adequate pay. Adequate pay arrives, nonetheless, in the astonishing codicil. Both Simonides and his "savior" have bestowed on one another a gift immeasurable in market terms. Their transaction is governed by God and generates a surplus value that far exceeds its own calculus.[51]

"Grace" (χάρις) is the almost untranslatable last word and final reckoning of Simonides' epitaphic commerce. Grace is the strange and impetuous currency of his transaction. Grace buys salvation in several directions at once, for it is an interchange of life and death embedded in the poet's function and coordinate with his avarice. A poet is someone who traffics in survival, reinflecting the fact of death into immortal publicity. Yet the dead man is not the only one who profits. It is Simonides' name that appears on this tombstone. It is we who find compensation in his poetic gift. Congealed in our poetic pleasure are the works of his life and the warrant of his salvation. Who saves the savior? "A hanged man strangles the rope," as Paul Celan says in an early poem.[52] Grace is a coin with more than two sides. In which we trust.

[50] Simonides fr. 85 *FGE; Palatine Anthology* 7.77.
[51] Surplus value is defined by Engels as "the product of labour for which its appropriator had not given any equivalent": Marx (1967), 2:15; by Marx as "a mere congelation of simple labour-time": (1967), 1.217; cf. 2:387ff.; Pilling (1980), 56–61.
[52] "Lob der Ferne": Celan (1983), 1:33.

CELAN

It is often said that money is like language. Marx thought this comparison weak. "Language does not transform ideas so that the peculiarity of ideas is dissolved and their social character runs alongside them as a separate entity, like prices alongside commodities. Ideas do not exist separately from language." Marx suggests an alternate model: money is not like language but it is like *translated* language. "Ideas which have first to be translated out of their mother tongue into a foreign (*fremde*) language in order to circulate, in order to become exchangeable, offer a somewhat better analogy. So the analogy lies not in language but in the foreign quality or strangeness (*Fremdheit*) of language."[53]

This simple striking notion, that money makes our daily life strange in the same way translation makes ordinary language strange, seems a helpful one for exploring the *Fremdheit* of Paul Celan. We have already seen how Simonides' alienation began with his historical situation—on a cusp between two economic systems, gazing at both and all too aware of their difference: like someone listening to simultaneous translation of a text that lies before him in the original. He is analogous to Paul Celan, after the model suggested by Marx, insofar as Celan is a poet who uses language *as if he were always translating*.

Strangeness for Celan arose out of language and went back down into language. The problem of translation has a special instance in him. For he lived in exile in Paris most of his life and wrote poetry in German, which was the language of his mother but also the language of those who murdered his mother. Born in a region of Romania that survived Soviet, then German, occupation, he moved to France in 1948 and lived there till his death. "As for me I am on the outside," he once said.[54] I don't think he meant by this (only) that he was a Romanian Jew with a French passport and a Christian wife, living in Paris and writing in Ger-

[53] Marx (1973), 80.
[54] Felstiner (1995), 94.

man. But rather that, in order to write poetry at all, he had to develop an outside relationship with a language he had once been inside. He had to reinvent German on the screen of itself, by treating his native tongue as a foreign language to be translated—into German. As Pierre Joris says, "German was . . . in an essential way, his *other* tongue. . . . Celan is estranged from that which is most familiar."[55] Nonetheless it was important to Celan to keep on in German. This passage from a speech he gave in Bremen has often been quoted:

> Erreichbar, nah und unverloren blieb inmitten der Verluste dies eine: die Sprache. Sie, die Sprache, blieb unverloren, ja, trotz allem. Aber sie mußte nun hindurchgehen durch ihre eigenen Antwortlosig-keiten, hindurchgehen durch furchtbares Verstummen, hindurch-gehen durch die tausend Finsternisse todbringender Rede. Sie ging hindurch und gab keine Worte her für das, was geschah; aber sie ging durch dieses Geschehen. Ging hindurch und durfte wieder zutage treten, "angereichert" von all dem.
>
> In dieser Sprache habe ich, in jenen Jahren und in den Jahren nachher, Gedichte zu schreiben versucht. . . .

> [Reachable, near and unlost amid the losses, this one thing remained: language. This thing, language, remained unlost, yes, in spite of every-thing. But it had to go through its own loss of answers, had to go through terrifying muteness, had to go through the thousand dark-nesses of deathbringing talk. It went through and gave no words for that which happened; yet it went through this happening. Went through and was able to come back to light "enriched" by it all.
>
> In this language I have tried, during those years and the years after, to write poems. . . .[56]]

Most critics hear in "thousand darknesses of deathbringing talk" a reference to the linguistic forms and usages of the Nazi regime. As Felstiner says:

[55] Joris (1995), 42.
[56] "Ansprache anläßlich der Entgegennahme des Literaturpreises der Freien Hansestadt Bremen (1958)": Celan (1990), 38; Waldrop (1986), 34.

29

For the Thousand-Year Reich organized its genocide of European Jewry by means of language: slogans, pseudo-scientific dogma, propaganda, euphemism, and the jargon that brought about every devastating "action" from the earliest racial "laws" through "special treatment" in the camps to the last "resettlement" of Jewish orphans.[57]

Surely the Nazis brought more death to the language than anyone else in its history. For Celan, to keep on in German despite this fact became the task of a lifetime. There is some suggestion, in a piece of prose he wrote in 1948 called "Edgar Jené and the Dream about the Dream," that he sometimes saw language-death as a more universal problem: the tendency of meanings to "burn out" of language and to be covered over by a "load of false and disfigured sincerity" is one that he here ascribes to "the whole sphere of human communicative means."[58] But let us note that he qualifies the phrase "load of false and disfigured sincerity" with an adjective, *tausendjährigen* ("thousand-year-long"), that combines an indefinite term for "age-old" with a glance at the Christian millennium and a reference to the Nazis in their fifteen minutes of fame. For Celan, I think, no philosophizing about language could escape this latter reference. It gives a context of "ashes" to everything he says.

Sprachgitter is a word Celan uses to describe the operations of his own poetic language, in a poem about strangeness and strangers. It is also the name of his third book of verse, published in 1959. The word is a compound of two nouns whose relation is ambivalent. *Sprach* refers to language; *Gitter* means some kind of lattice, fence or woven mesh. For people living cloistered lives, *Gitter* is the grillework or *fenestra locutaria* through which they speak to those outside. For fishermen, it means a net or trap. For mineralogists, the lattice formation of a crystal.[59] Does Celan use *Gitter* to imply passage, blockage or salvaging of speech? Mesh can do all of

---

[57] Felstiner (1995), xvii; for an eyewitness account of how the Nazis used language, see Klemperer (1995).

[58] "Edgar Jené und der Traum vom Traume": Celan (1990), 7–16; Waldrop (1986), 3–10.

[59] On this word, whose metaphorical use goes back to Jean Paul (1763–1825), see Bollack in Colin (1987), 113–56; Kelletat in Meinecke (1970), 116–35; Washburn and Guillemin (1986), xviii–xix.

these. Celan may mean all of these. Like Simonides' munificent host Hieron, the German language offers Celan a qualified hospitality, a murderously impure meal. Remember how Simonides took it upon himself to "keep a small portion and sell the rest" of the food sent to him by Hieron. Celan can make himself at home in his mother tongue only by a process of severe and parsimonious redaction. Simonides' name for his own parsimony was κοσμιότης: "sense of order" or "decorum, decency." Celan sees himself ordering language through mesh. Mesh limits what he can say but may also cleanse it. As crystal it cleanses to the essence. As net it salvages what is cleansed.

"Sprachgitter" is a poem that both describes and demonstrates how a mesh for language works:[60]

SPRACHGITTER

Augenrund zwischen den Stäben.

Flimmertier Lid
rudert nach oben,
gibt einen Blick frei.

Iris, Schwimmerin, traumlos und trüb:
der Himmel, herzgrau, muß nah sein.

Schräg, in der eisernen Tülle,
der blakende Span.
Am Lichtsinn
errätst du die Seele.

(Wär ich wie du. Wärst du wie ich.
Standen wir nicht
unter *einem* Passat?
Wir sind Fremde.)

Die Fliesen. Darauf,
dicht beieinander, die beiden
herzgrauen Lachen:

[60] Celan (1983), 1:167

31

zwei
Mundvoll Schweigen.

[LANGUAGE MESH

Eyeround between the bars.
Glimmeranimal lid
rows upward,
sets a look free.

Iris, swimmer, dreamless and dismal:
the sky, heartgrey, must be near.

Slanted, in the iron socket,
the smoking splinter.
By its lightsense
you guess the soul.

(Were I like you. Were you like me.
Stand we not
under *one* tradewind?
We are strangers.)

The pavingstones. On them,
tight by each other, the two
heartgrey pools:
two
mouthsfull of silence.]

This poem works like a mesh. In it you see an eye behind bars and
a glance that gets through. You look down the glance and see
deeper, inside the eye, to an iris that swims there, to a splinter that
smokes there, and to a conjecture (from light) of the presence of
soul. *Seele* is the furthest in you can go: the poem flicks you sud-
denly out of the mesh—into a parenthesis where the external
facts of your relationship with *ich* are noted. Sudden strangeness
is stated as a contrafactual condition between *ich* and *du*, who
stand side by side, yet alien. Although I have just glimpsed your
soul, we are strangers. Our alienation looks (from outside: on the
pavingstones) like two pools of water that lie side by side, as close

as two eyes.[61] Pools reflect the sky ("heartgrey . . . heartgrey") but are speechless: two mouthsfull of silence.

The action of the poem, as it pulls you deep in and then thrusts you out of the mesh that is *ich,* the mesh that is *Sprachgitter,* moves with the springy recoil of a bad conversation and cleanses us of the illusion that we could talk.[62] The parenthesis in the middle is a shock: like Simonides' decision to sell food, it turns the values of the situation inside out and leaves the harsh decorum of strangers suddenly exposed.

An action of estrangement, then, takes place in this poem between *ich* and *du:* it is an ordering action. An image (of two eyes) passes through its mesh and becomes another image (of two pools). Your glimpse of my soul becomes our contiguous silences. I have suggested that this poetic action represents, in some part, the condition of intimate alienation that obtained between Celan and his own language. I would also suggest that for Celan, as for Simonides, such alienation contoured his relations with other people. He traveled to the houses of the great and there found *Fremdheit.*

Not Undelayed

Occasions of hospitality are as critical to Celan's biography as they were in the life story of Simonides. To find himself "standing under one wind" with people who turned out to be "strangers" was a recurrent experience that marked Celan's hopes and entered into his verse. Let us consider two of these occasions, his meeting with Martin Buber in 1960 and his visit to Martin Heidegger in 1967.

Celan's pilgrimage to Heidegger's hut at Todtnauberg has been the subject of much documentation and analysis.[63] He must

[61] Cf. Danton, diene Lippen haben Augen!: Dantons Tod 1.5: Büchner (1922).

[62] Cf. Gottfried Benn's discussion of poetic consciousness as a "perforated" thing, a "mesh-I," in his essay "Probleme der Lyrik": Das lyrische Ich ist ein durchbrochenes Ich, ein Gitter-Ich: (1968), 1.512; Glenn (1973), 100–104.

[63] Baumann (1986), 58–80; Felstiner (1995), 244–47; Golb (1988); Hamburger (1990); Joris in Block (1991), 61–68; Lacoue-Labarthe (1986), 130–53; Pöggeler (1986), 240–56.

have come to Heidegger hungry for answers to some pertinent political questions; whether or not he got to ask these questions is unclear from his own poetic account of the event ("Todtnauberg"). Most commentators read Celan's inscription in Heidegger's guestbook—"Into the hutbook, looking at the wellstar, with a hope for a coming word in the heart"—as the record of a disappointed hope, and see his poem "Todtnauberg" as pointedly organized around "an emptiness or silence at its approximate center."[64] Heidegger had long been a master of "the danger-free privilege of silence" (to borrow a phrase from Simonides)[65] and his mastery was apparently unshaken by Celan's poem, which Celan sent to Heidegger in a special bibliophile edition soon after their meeting; Heidegger responded with a letter of conventional thanks. When the poem appeared in Celan's next book, a verse had been altered. From "a hope today of a thinking man's (undelayed coming) word in the heart," Celan removed the word "undelayed."

Delay, disappointment and hunger are experiences catalytic for poets. When Simonides went to dine with Hieron, he had to complain of hare and snow withheld. We saw these deprivations moved him to compose two poems that comment on the erosion of the ancient host/guest convention and parody the hollow diction in which relations between *xenoi* may come to be framed, once money replaces love in the structure of the event. When Celan went to visit Martin Buber, he experienced deep moral disappointment in the encounter and composed a poem about the "loss" and "salvaging" of certain words. Felstiner summarizes what went wrong with the encounter:

> Buber came to Paris in September 1960. . . . Celan, just back from his comfortless visit with Nelly Sachs in Stockholm, telephoned and went to Buber's hotel on 13 September. He took his copies of Buber's books to be signed and actually kneeled for a blessing from the 82-year-old patriarch. But the homage miscarried. How had it felt (Celan wanted to know) after the catastrophe, to go on writing in German

---

[64] Golb (1988), 257.
[65] Simonides fr. 582 *PMG;* Aristides *Orationes* 3.96.

and publishing in Germany? Buber evidently demurred, saying it was natural to publish there and taking a pardoning stance toward Germany. Celan's vital need, to hear some echo of his plight, Buber could not or would not grasp.[66]

After he came away from Buber, Celan wrote this poem:[67]

DIE SCHLEUSE

Über aller dieser deiner
Trauer: kein
zweiter Himmel.

. . . . . .

An einen Mund,
dem es ein Tausendwort war,
verlor—
verlor ich ein Wort,
das mir verblieben war:
Schwester.

An die Vielgötterei
verlor ich ein Wort, das mich suchte:
Kaddisch.

Durch
die Schleuse mußt ich,
das Wort in die Salzflut zurück—
und hinaus—und hinüberzuretten:
Jiskor.

[THE SLUICE

Over all this grief
of yours: no
second heaven.

. . . . . .

To a mouth,
for which it was a thousandword,

---

66 Felstiner (1995), 161.
67 Celan (1983), 1:222.

lost—
I lost a word,
that had remained to me:
sister.

To
manygoddedness
I lost a word that was looking for me:
Kaddish.

Through
the sluice I had to go,
to salvage the word into the saltflood back
and out and across:
Yizkor.]

The poem talks of two words lost, one saved. "Sister" may refer generally to kinsmen dead in the war,[68] or specifically to Celan's dear friend Nelly Sachs, who was in mental disarray and who had refused to see Celan when he went to Stockholm to visit her in hospital at the beginning of September 1960.[69] The word *Kaddish* is Aramaic for "holy" and the name of a Jewish prayer recited by relatives of a dead person. If these two words are lost to Celan, so is the expectation of conventional human or religious comfort. He is describing a grief that no current ideas of kinship or redemption can cover. The line of dots in the fourth verse (after "no second heaven") obliterates any glance a poet might think to cast at the sky in hope of an option. Nonetheless, without option, comfort or worship, an action remains to him—the same action named in the title of the book *Sprachgitter.* The poet's act is to cleanse words and to salvage what is cleansed. "Through the sluice I had to go. . . ." Through the sluice he goes to save *Yizkor.* It is a Hebrew word for "May God Remember" and also the name

---

[68] Cf. Celan's poem "Chymisch" in which the word *Schwestergestalt* ("sister shape") is placed in apposition to *Alle die Namen, alle die mitverbrannten Namen* ("All the names, all those names burnt with the rest"): Celan (1983), 1:227; Hamburger (1989), 179.

[69] Felstiner (1995), 161.

of a memorial service that begins with this prayer. *Yizkor*, like *Kaddish*, remembers the dead, but the history and character of the two prayers are different. For *Kaddish* was not originally associated with mourning or death and is in fact a prayer of praise, offered by a mourner who rises in public, despite his grief, to bless God's name.[70] *Kaddish* is recited as an affirmation of faith in God's judgment, in the face of death, after the manner of Job, who cried out, "Though He slay me yet will I trust him" (*Job* 13:15). This word of trust and praise is lost to Celan. But he has kept hold of *Yizkor*. When I asked my friend Rabbi Horowitz about *Yizkor*, this is what he said:

> *Yizkor*, the memorial service for the deceased, follows the Haftorah. Its origin is obscure. It is mentioned in Parashat Ha'azinu in the Midrash and in Machzor Vitry (p. 173). It was originally introduced as a prayer only for Yom Kippur, to remind people of the importance of prayer by recalling man's final destiny on this earth. At the time of the Crusades, when many thousands of Jews were murdered by the fanatical crusaders, it assumed additional meaning as an expression of sorrow for the Jewish people as a whole. In our generation, a special prayer has been added to memorialize the six million martyrs of the Holocaust. Later, *Yizkor* was introduced on Sh'mini Ateseret, on the last day of Pesach, and on the second day of Sha'vu'ot. It is a sad commentary on the state of "religion" in the Diaspora that many Jews, who do not even attend services, rush to the synagogue for the sole purpose of reciting *Yizkor*. I sadly refer to them as "Yizkor Jews."[71]

Yizkor seems to be a word that has deep historical attachment and a particular relationship to memory. *Kaddish*, although used for commemorative purpose, is not essentially a word of memory but rather a word that covers over the memory of human loss with praise of God's glory. *Yizkor* does not cover over, it insists on remembering; indeed it insists that God do the remembering alongside us, Yizkor Jews and all.

---

[70] It was originally a prayer that followed the words of a teacher in a house of study and is first mentioned as a prayer of mourning by Rabbi Yitzchak Ben Moshe of Vienna (1180–1260) in his book *Or Zaru'a*, so Rabbi Horowitz tells me.

[71] Horowitz (1985), 39.

What is remembering? Remembering brings the absent into the present, connects what is lost to what is here. Remembering draws attention to lostness and is made possible by emotions of space that open backward into a void. Memory depends on void, as void depends on memory, to think it. Once void is thought, it can be cancelled. Once memory is thought, it can be commodified. Simonides of Keos first made these relationships clear in his invention of the famous Simonidean "art of memory." Let us consider the events that led up to his invention.

MEMORY

Skopas, perhaps the most ungracious of Simonides' patrons, was a prince of the Skopad family of Thessaly. From scattered references in the scholia, it appears that Simonides lived for some time in Thessaly, composing and performing poems at Krannon and Pharsalos, the seats of the Skopadai, and also at Larisa, home of the Aleuadai.[72] The terms of Simonides' contracts with these patrons may be inferred from remarks of the poet Theokritos, whose Sixteenth Idyll describes the workings of a great Thessalian house of that era, and from a passage in Cicero's *De oratore* where the orator recounts a day in the life of Simonides at Skopas' home. As usual in Simonides' life story, the two sources give us a bifocal view of the poet's economic situation. From Theokritos we get an idealized picture of ancient *xenia* in which wealthy and hospitable householders exchange goods and services with a number of loyal retainers:

> Many in the houses of Antiochos and King Aleuas were the workers
>   who received the allotted monthly measure of food.
> Many were the Skopad calves driven to fold
>   alongside the horned cattle bellowing.
> And ten thousand on the plain of Krannon were the flocks
>   that shepherds drove into open air for the hospitable Kreondai.

[72] On Simonides among the Thessalians, see Van Groningen (1948).

But hospitality had other constituents, Theokritos emphasizes, in the relations between householder and poet:

The fact is there would be no joy at all for them [the Skopads],
    once they emptied their sweet soul into the hateful old man's
    boat:
unremembered—though they left behind that whole great wealth of
    theirs—
    would they lie long ages
among the miserable dead, had the divine singer of Keos
    not lifted up the ravishing palette of his voice
and named their names for men to come.[73]

The ideal of this contract is clear: the Skopads sustain Simonides on earth, he sustains them in memory. An exchange of life for life. Of mortal for immortal continuance. You might think it a delicate matter to price such a commodity. Cicero gives us a more realistic picture of how Skopas went about it:

Once Simonides was dining at Krannon in Thessaly at the house of the rich and noble Skopas. He had composed a song in honor of this man and in it he put a lot of typical ornamental material concerning Kastor and Polydeukes. Whereat Skopas ungenerously declared that he would pay Simonides only half the fee they had agreed on for the song: the other half he should get from the gods whom he had praised to that extent. Just then Simonides received a message that two young men were asking for him at the front door on a matter of urgent business. He got up and went out but found no one there. Meanwhile the roof of the room in which Skopas was dining collapsed, killing him and his friends. Now when the kinsfolk of these people wished to bury them, they found it impossible to recognize the remains. But Simonides, it is said, by remembering the exact place where each man had sat at the table, was able to identify them all for

---

[73] Theokritos *Idylls* 16.34–39 and 40–46. It may seem unsound to cite Cicero and Theokritos, who are after all harking back from centuries later to an icon of Simonides' life and times derived entirely from literature and literary gossip. But this icon is our subject. Simonides began it. Tolstoy really did die waiting for a train.

burial. From this he discovered that it is order that mainly contributes to memory its light. . . . I am grateful to Simonides of Keos who thus invented (so they say) the art of memory.[74]

The anecdote quivers with allegory throughout, but especially when Cicero says, "I am grateful" (*gratiam habeo*). His word for gratitude is *gratia* (χάρις in Greek, "grace" in English). Let us take it as referring to the whole fund of grace that flows back and forth between a poet and his world. Simonides' salvific action—both the particular act of remembering certain names and the wider gift of an *ars memoria* to the world—is a paradigm of what the poet does in confrontation with void. He thinks it and he thanks it, we could say (borrowing a phrase from Paul Celan's Bremen speech),[75] for it is the beginning of an immeasurable moment of value. Skopas mistook this and halved Simonides' fee, as if to insist that poetic action has an exact equivalent in cash. We may read a degree of divine disapproval in the collapse of the roof and appearance of the Dioskouroi at the door. And here the allegory takes a wry turn. For the Dioskouroi are gods who know better than anyone else the cost of halving.

According to myth, Kastor and Polydeukes are brothers (one mortal, the other immortal) who could not bear to be parted by death and so divide a single eternity between them, spending alternate days on and under the earth, infinitely half-lost. "Now they are living, day and day about," says Homer.[76] Mortality and immortality continue side by side in them, hinged by a strange arrangement of grace. A poet is also a sort of hinge. Through songs of praise he arranges a continuity between mortal and immortal life for a man like Skopas. And although Skopas believes he is paying Simonides a certain price for a certain quantity of words, in fact he acquires a memory that will prolong him far beyond all these. He will be one of the unlost. Gratitude is in order.

[74] Cicero *De oratore* 2.86.
[75] Celan (1990), 37; Waldrop (1986), 33 and below.
[76] *Odyssey* 11.301ff.; cf. *Iliad* 3.243ff.; *Kypria* fr. 6 Allen; Alkman fr. 7 *PMG;* Pindar *Pythians* 11.61–64; *Nemeans* 10.49–91.

Gratitude and memory go together, morally and philologically. Paul Celan locates memory, in his Bremen speech, in an etymological link between thinking and thanking:

Denken und Danken sind in unserer Sprache Worte ein und desselben Ursprungs. Wer ihrem Sinn folgt, begibt sich in den Bedeutungsbereich von: "gedenken," "engedenk sein," "Andenken," "Andacht."

[To Think and to Thank are in our language words of one and the same origin. Whoever follows their sense comes to the semantic field of "to remember," "to be mindful," "memory," "devotion."][77]

For the Greeks, memory is rooted in utterance, if we may judge from the etymology of the noun μνήμη ("memory"), which is cognate with the verb μιμνήσκομαι ("I remember," "I make mention," "I name"), and from the genealogy of the goddess Mnemosyne, who is called "mother of the Muses" by Homer and Hesiod.[78] Memorable naming is the function of poetry, within a society like that of the Greeks, for the poet uses memory to transform our human relationship to time. Had Simonides not named their names, the Skopads would have vanished into the past. As a poet he is under contract to say something that will continue the Skopad memory for as long as his words can charm our attention. Skopas treats this contract as a stark exchange of couplets for coins, but surely there is a difference—a difference to memorability—between being named (say) as an actuarial statistic on the evening news and being transformed by the ravishing palette of Simonides' voice into a song of praise. A difference hard to quantify.

[77] Celan (1990), 37; Waldrop (1986), 33. Celan does not specify the sources of his reflection on these matters; nonetheless, see *Erläuterungen zu Hölderlins Dichtung* (Frankfurt 1981) on Heidegger's development of the concept of remembrance in his reading of Hölderlin's "Andenken"; on relations between thought, memory and thanks: *Was heißt Denken?* (Tübingen 1962), 91–95; Fynsk in Fioretos (1994), 160 and 181 n. 2.
[78] *Homeric Hymn to Hermes* 429; Hesiod *Theogony* 54.

Memory has a starkly quantitative aspect, of which Simonides shows his mastery when he mentally reconstitutes Skopas' dinner table. This is the *ars memoria* so admired by Cicero and others.[79] But memory has another aspect (hinted in Cicero's *gratia*), which the Greeks called divine and which comes through the poet like a light shed on darkening things. This diviner aspect resists quantification; nonetheless, it makes the difference between oblivion and fame, between dead body and living name, for Skopas and all his guests. Simonides knows how to connect these two aspects of memory, by a power of mind that the gods underwrite when Skopas declines to pay. Simonides creates a moment of order.

"Order" is the main mechanism of the Simonidean mnemonic system, according to Cicero, who uses the Latin word *ordo* ("order," "exact positioning," "arrangement") to describe Simonides' technique of visualizing data in fixed position like guests around a table. If it were translated into Greek, *ordo* would become κόσμος (*kosmos*), the principle that Simonides invoked once in Syrakuse to explain why he sold gifts of food from Hieron: "So that Hieron's munificence may be truly visible, *not to mention my own sense of order* (κοσμιότης)." What does a poet's "sense of order" comprehend?

The Greek word *kosmos* can denote many kinds of order—planetary, governmental, social, sartorial, linguistic—as if all the different strands of human and natural complication in the world were woven out of one texture, extending over both space and time. As he lingers on the doorstep of what had been Skopas' house and stares at the smoking ruin of the dining hall, Simonides is contemplating a piece of the texture that now exists nowhere but in his own mind. This is true in several ways at once. Visualizing a dining hall where guests sit side by side enjoying Skopas' hospitality, does he not also evoke the whole archaic convention of *xenia* whose decorums he has seen gradually disintegrating, throughout his professional career, under the dull impact of money? When he names the names of all the obliterated

---

[79] The Parian Marble 54 chronicles the invention of a mnemonic system as chief among Simonides' achievements; see also Suidas s.v. *Simonides;* Kallimachos *Aitia* 21; Cicero *De finibus* 2.32; Quintilian *Institutio oratoria* 11.2.11.

guests, does he not exceed his original contract with Skopas by an act of grace that recalls precisely those sentiments of reciprocal *philia* in which hospitality was traditionally nurtured? Aristotle says that the wife of Hieron once asked Simonides whether it is better to be wise or rich. "Rich! For I see the wise lingering on the doorsteps of the rich," declared the poet.[80] The answer is a bleak one. Simonides had some experience of doorsteps. And he could remember a time when wisdom was not so marginal.

"As to memory, I say nobody can equal Simonides!" said Simonides at the age of eighty.[81] The poet does not just *use* memory, he *embodies* it. We could say that use value and exchange value fuse in this commodity, but in fact Simonides' "sense of order" is more than an entrepreneurial impulse. His alienation flows open as experience and paradigm. His memory construct, unlike later mnemotechnic methods, is not artificial: Simonides had sat in the room that becomes his theater of memory, he ate dinner amidst the data.[82] This poet is someone caught between two worlds, remembering both. His flame in every grain. For him, memory is both commodity and gift, both wage and grace.

In Paul Celan's German, poetic order is a function of the "language mesh" that separates, cleanses, traps, keeps words. When Celan says, in the Bremen speech, that the German language has come back to day "enriched" by its passage through events and time, he too is blending experience and paradigm into a method of memory.[83] The method is not artificial, it is lived—fluctuating in strange grace like Kastor and Polydeukes, replacing death with certain salvaged words, day and day about. Six times in the Bremen speech he uses the verb *hindurchgehen,* "to go through," of the salvaging of language into memory. His poem "Die Schleuse"

[80] Aristotle *Rhetoric* 1391a.

[81] Aristides *Orationes* 28.59.

[82] On the history and use of mnemotechnic systems, see Rose (1993); Spence (1985); Yates (1966).

[83] Lyon (1974) sees in the verb, which Celan sets in quotation marks, a technical term from mining: "It denotes a specific chemical process which takes place in bodies of ore such as copper or silver that lie buried in the earth. These ore bodies can become "enriched" when other materials enter and form chemical concentrations that raise their yield" (298).

represents the poet himself "going through" a sluice to get back *Yizkor*. Why this word? *Yizkor* constitutes in itself an act of human memory yet it also implicates God—not in a praising or trusting or comforting way, but attentively. *May He Remember.* A word waiting for the knock of the Dioskouroi at the door. Still.

CHAPTER II

Visibles Invisibles

SIMONIDES

Money is something visible and invisible at the same time. A "real abstraction," in Marx's terms. You can hold a coin in your hand and yet not touch its value. That which makes this thing "money" is not what you see.[1] When the ancient Greeks talk of money, adjectives for "visible" and "invisible" occur inconsistently. Money can be found categorized as "invisible" when contrasted with real estate, for example; as "visible" when it means a bank deposit that is part of an inheritance.[2] Modern scholars have been unsuccessful in efforts to abstract a stable definition for these terms from ancient usage.[3] In the view of the anthropologist Louis Gernet, the confusion represents a "flawed category" created by the Greeks when they tried to fit the many nuances of moneyed situations into a binary terminology. "The problem is, thought moves in many directions."[4] Money also moves in many directions. Simonides, we know, had occasion to observe these movements and to meditate on their relation to the phenomena of perception. He lived at an interface between two economic systems. His texts and testimonia make clear that he gave thought to the concepts of visible and invisible, was aware of a turmoil in their categorization and had an interest (conditioned perhaps by economic experience) in their valuing.[5] This interest shows up especially in his statements about what poetry is and how it works. He seems to believe that the visible and invisible worlds lie side by side—may

[1] Cf. Marx (1867), 1:73, 567–68; Sohn-Rethel (1978), 6.

[2] See LSJ *s.v.* and Gernet (1968), 343–47.

[3] "It was the persistence of the counterpoised categories, not the 'true' nature of the objects that determined classification": Cohen (1992), 193.

[4] Gernet (1968), 345.

[5] Cf. Marx: "Money is the external common medium and faculty for transforming appearance into reality and reality into appearance": Struik (1964), 153.

be interchangeable. Which of the two you notice is up to you. No lines just break off.

ICONOLOGY

Simonides is Western culture's original literary critic, for he is the first person in our extant tradition to theorize about the nature and function of poetry. The central dictum of his literary critical theory is well known, much celebrated and little understood. "Simonides says that painting is silent poetry while poetry is painting that talks," Plutarch tells us.[6] What did the poet mean? Why did Simonides choose to inaugurate literary criticism by setting his own verbal art against the ground of painting?

It is true he was a most painterly poet, using proportionately more color words than any writer of his time and congratulated by Longinus for his pictorial power (εἰδωλοποίησε).[7] His poems are well described as miniature canvases where each word is as meticulously placed as a brushstroke. In real life he seems to have enjoyed the society and patronage of painters, as a composer of inscriptions to identify art works on public display, for example, the sensational *Iliupersis* painted by Polygnotos at Delphi.[8] Perhaps it

[6] Plutarch *Moralia* 346–47; see also 17–18, 58b. The comparison between poetry and painting figures in the theoretical discourse of the author of the *Dissoi logoi* 3.10; Plato *Republic* 605a; *Cratylus* 425a, 430b–e, 432d; Aristotle *Poetics* 47a, 50a, 50b, 54b, 60b; Horace *Ars poetica* 361–65; Cicero *Disputationes Tusculanae* 5.39.114; Longinus *De sublimitate* 17.20; Dio Chrysostom *Olympics 12;* Augustine *In Ioannis Evangelium* 24.2; Leonardo da Vinci *Treatise on Painting;* McMahon (1956), 11–21; and surfaces regularly in the arguments of later aestheticians from Lessing (1766) to McLuhan (1968). Secondary discussions include Alpers (1972); Atkins (1934); Bell (1978); Brink (1971); Burke (1757); Dorsch (1977); Du Bos (1740); Hagstrum (1958); Harriott (1969); Hazlitt (1844); Hermeren (1969); Lee (1940); Markiewicz (1987); Panofsky (1939); Schapiro (1973); Thayer (1975); Trimpi (1973); Uspensky (1972); Van Hook (1905); Wellek (1942); Wimsatt (1954); Wolfe (1975).

[7] Longinus *De sublimitate* 15.7.

[8] Pausanias tell us of the Polygnotan inscription (10.25.1), while Plutarch cites Simonides as an authority on the paintings in the town hall at Phlya (*Life of*

46

was this association that inspired Simonides to formulate in such starkly iconologic terms his own philosophy of art, in the famous fragment:

ὁ λόγος τῶν πραγμάτων εἰκών ἐστιν.[9]

[The word is a picture of things.]

At any rate, he must have felt he had something to learn from what painters were doing, or from what people in his day were saying and thinking about painting. So let us consider what that was.

Inarguably, Simonides lived at a time when no thinking man could ignore what was going on in painting. As Pliny tell us, during this period "the art of painting set itself apart."[10] The fifth century B.C. saw a handful of Greek artists utterly revolutionize existing notions of the pictorial field, in a way that proved decisive not just for Greek art but for the whole subsequent history of European painting. Polygnotos and the generation of painters that followed him took as their starting point the two-dimensional picture plane of archaic style and developed a new technology for the representation of three-dimensional reality. With the invention of techniques like foreshortening, linear perspective, mixing and gradation of colors, superposition of paints and patching of surfaces, as well as various kinds of proportional adjustment for optical illusion, these painters transformed flat surface into an illusory world of objects moving in space.[11] They generated a body of technical data based on the parallel classification of painting and literature, which is standard still in our discourse about art. After the Polygnotan revolution, painters were no longer decorators of surfaces but magicians who conjured the real world upon the viewer's eye.

Themistokles 1.4). Simonides also found occasion to mention, in a now-unknown context, a painter of Rhegium named Sillax (fr. 634 *PMG*).

[9] Michael Psellos fr. 821 Migne.

[10] Pliny *Natural History* 35.29. See further Bruno (1977), 1–30; Keuls (1978), 3, 58–61; Robertson (1959), 111–36; Swindler (1929), 196–236.

[11] Keuls (1978), 2–5, 58–65; Gombrich (1968), 40.

APATĒ

The new science of three-dimensional representation created shockwaves that were felt far beyond Polygnotos' paintbrush. "Painting is philosophy," said Leonardo da Vinci, speaking from a culture confident in the painter's power to transcribe reality.[12] But ancient Greek culture registered a rather different response to the development of illusionism in art. We find one index of this in the vehemence with which Plato denounces painters and painting throughout his dialogues. For Plato, painting is not philosophy but sophistry, an art form devoted to replacing life with the lifelike and truth with what is convincing. "They create phantasms not reality" (φαντάσματα οὐκ ὄντα), he says, comparing painters with sophists as practitioners of a "phantastical technique" (φανταστικὴ τέχνη) whose product is "a sort of man-made dream created for those who are awake."[13] Plato's quarrel is not with painting itself so much as with the use of any representational medium to defraud reality. By virtue of its power of deception, painting is analogous with sophistic rhetoric and also with the art of mimetic poetry, in Plato's view: these three modes of illusion share a common delight in their own capacity to trick, dissemble and beguile.[14] The term that came to be used for this capacity in the critical discourse of the fifth century was ἀπάτη: "deception," "illusion," "trickery". The pursuit and perfection of ἀπάτη (*apatē*), the art of deception, was an explicit feature of sophistic aesthetic theory, both visual and verbal.

"The best painter or poet is the one who does the most deceiving," says the anonymous sophist who composed the *Dissoi logoi*,[15] and, we are informed by Gorgias, "the word (λόγος) that tricks

[12] Holt (1957), 1:277.

[13] Plato *Republic* 599a; *Sophist* 234, 266c7–9.

[14] On the relation Plato discerned or thought he discerned between poetry and sophistry, see Robinson (1987), 259–66.

[15] Fr. 3.10 *VS*. Cf. the author's citations from Aiskhylos (3.12) and Kleoboulinos (3.11); Plato *Republic* 596d–e. See further Freeman (1946), 417–19; Rosenmeyer (1965), 234; Robinson (1987).

you is more just than the λόγος that does not."[16] That trickery and illusion, or ἀπάτη, are somehow inherent in λόγος was an insight at least as old as Homer and Hesiod, which the sophists pursued to its logical extension.[17] Teachers like Gorgias and Protagoras alleged that the proper activity of words is not to describe but to deceive and erected on this basis a pungent philosophy of language as well as a lucrative program of professional instruction, advertising themselves as educational successors to the ancient poets.[18] Plato deplored the profession for the same reason that he deplored poetry all the way back to Homer, namely, that it cut words free from any obligation to reality. "Λόγος is its own master, a great δυνάστης" ("tyrant" or "power-monger") able to "make all things its slaves." So Gorgias tells us.[19] It remains to be seen whether an ancient poet would have endorsed this tyrannical conception of words and how they work.

Situated between Polygnotos and Protagoras, Simonides was in a position to appreciate the impact made on the Greek popular imagination by illusionism, visual and verbal. Although older than the older sophists, Simonides anticipated their intellectual concerns so accurately that he has been designated a "proto-sophist" by critics modern and ancient.[20] Furthermore, Simonides was the first person in recorded Greek usage to employ the term ἀπάτη in its literary critical sense as "artistic illusion."[21] Yet Simonides

[16] Fr. B23 *VS* = Plutarch *Moralia* 348c; cf. Gorgias fr. B11.17–18 *VS*.

[17] Even Homer's Zeus resorts to a silent nod of the head when he wishes to make an "undeceiving" (οὐδ᾽ ἀπατηλὸν, *Iliad* 1.526) assertion, while Hesiod's Muses exult in their authority over truth and lies at once (*Theogony* 27): cf. *Homeric Hymn to Hermes* 4.560–63; Solon fr. 29 West; Parmenides fr. B8.50–52; B19 *VS*. Further on ἀπάτη, see Bell (1978), 81–82; Christ (1941), 41–48; Detienne (1981), 106–43; Heinimann (1945), 39–47; Hoffman (1925); Van Groningen (1948), 1–7; Luther (1935), 80–92; Pohlenz (1920), 169; Rosenmeyer (1965), 227–30; Rostagni (1922), 78; Snell (1926), 355–69; Suss (1910), 52–60; Untersteiner (1949), 1.184–85; 2.68.

[18] Guthrie (1969), 3.42–45.

[19] Fr. B11.8–14 *VS;* Plato *Philebus* 58a–b.

[20] Plato *Protagoras* 316d; Christ (1941), 41; Rosenmeyer (1965), 233; Thayer (1975), 10; Wilamowitz-Moellendorf (1913), 141.

[21] In an anecdote (whose structure and tone may suggest the usage was al-

49

could not, I think, have meant the same thing the sophists meant by ἀπάτη, nor accepted the severe critique of poetic function implied in their theory and practice of language as necessary deception.[22]

The sophists taught an art of persuasion that subsumed poetry to itself as one of several techniques useful for implanting opinions in the soul of a listener. Poetry, said Gorgias, is just "prose dressed up in meter,"[23] an artifact distinctive by virtue of its surface, not its content. He denied to λόγος in general any power to penetrate appearances: "The beauty of things unseen cannot be expressed in words," he asserted.[24] Like the illusionist painter, the sophist is interested in nothing not visible on his canvas. "Some representations are better than others but none is truer," says a Protagorean young person in Plato's *Theatetus.* Or, as Leonardo da Vinci put it, "Paint extends only to the surface of bodies."[25] Illusionism, in paint as in words, appears to have been at issue in the fifth century B.C. because it entails a total investment in the visible surface of the world as reality and a tendency to disavow the reality of anything not visible. Facts are all that matter and the facts are what you see. Among fifth-century painters, it was Zeuxis who most sensationally mastered the facts of illusionism. He is said to have rendered a bunch of grapes so realistically that birds flew down to peck at the canvas.[26] Among fifth-century sophists, it was Protagoras who most suavely formulated the philosophy of visible facts in his well-known dictum, "Man is the measure of all

---

ready commonplace) Plutarch records that, when asked why he did not bother "to deceive the Thessalians," Simonides replied, "The Thessalians are too stupid to be deceived by me" (Plutarch *Moralia* 15d). We should note, but not concede, Wilamowitz's claim that the witticism is too natty for Simonides and deserves transfer to Gorgias: (1913), 143.

[22] On sophistic appraisal of the value of poetry, see Gomme (1954), 55–78; Jaeger (1945) 1.296; Pohlenz (1920), 162–63, 178; Webster (1939), 171; Woodbury (1953), 137.

[23] Frr. B23 and B11.9 *VS;* cf. Plato *Gorgias* 502c.

[24] Fr. B28 *VS*. The Gorgian attribution is disputed: see Freeman (1946), 366; but the thought seems in no way foreign to a fifth-century intellectual mood typified by Gorgias.

[25] Plato *Theatetus* 167b; McMahon (1956), 90.

[26] Pliny *Natural History* 35.66; cf. Plato *Republic* 598c.

things, both of the things that are, that they are, and of the things that are not, that they are not." Sextus Empiricus cites this fragment for us and goes on to explain it in these terms:

Διὰ τοῦτο τίθησι τὰ φαινόμενα ἑκάστωι μόνα καὶ οὕτως εἰσάγει τὸ πρός τι.[27]

[In this way (Protagoras) posits only what is visible to each person and so introduces relativity.]

Protagorean relativity was a man-made dream to which Simonides would not have subscribed, as he made clear when he defined poetry by its difference from painting. For there is one thing a poem can do that a painting cannot, and in an age of sophistry and illusionism it is a thing of transforming importance, namely, render the invisible: Simonides' iconology captures not only bird and grapes but also the stingy fact of the picture frame that separates them. His commitment is to a reality beyond "what is visible to each person." His medium is words positioned so as to lead you to the edge where words stop, pointing beyond themselves toward something no eye can see and no painter can paint.

It is a rendering technique best observed at close range. Let us reconsider, in literal transcription, the celebrated Simonidean sentence cited above:

ὁ λόγος τῶν πραγμάτων εἰκών ἐστιν.

[The word of things a picture is.]

True to itself, the statement does what it says. It shows us λόγος and εἰκών poised on either side of the world of τῶν πραγμάτων in a syntactic tension that precisely pictures their ontology. "Things," in the genitive case, depend for their meaning on "word" and "picture" at once: both nominatives vie for the attention of the genitive πραγμάτων, which is placed to read in either direction and unite all three words like the hinge of a backsprung bow.[28] It is a taut and

27 Protagoras fr. A3 *VS*.
28 The backsprung bow is a figure introduced by Simonides' contemporary, the philosopher Heraklitos, in a controversial fragment. "They do not understand how that which differs is of one sense with itself: backstretched (παλίν-

self-controlled construction, but not self-sufficient. The verb ἐστιν ("is") secures the relationship from outside, even though, in such a sentence in Greek, the verb "is" is redundant. Simonides' ἐστιν insists on itself after other words have had their say and extraneous to their needs. Why? Simonides seems to want to paint more than words need to say. His iconic grammar renders a relationship that is mutual, dynamic and deeper than the visible surface of the language. As a painter who uses words to make paintings, Simonides requires of his reader a different kind of attention than we normally pay to verbal surfaces. It is a mode of attention well described by the Chinese painter Chiang Te Li, who wrote a treatise in the ninth century A.D. on how to do plum blossom. "Painting plum blossom is like buying a horse," says Chiang Te Li; "you go by bone structure not by appearances."[29] When we consider Simonidean sentences, we see appearances engaged in a dialectic with one another, by participation of λόγος and εἰκὼν at once. We overhear a conversation that sounds like reality. No other Greek writer of the period, except perhaps Heraklitos, uses the sentence in this way, as a "synthetic and tensional"[30] unit that reenacts the reality of which it speaks. This is mimesis in its most radical mechanism. This is the bone structure of poetic deception.

Leonidas

Simonides puts radical mimesis to use as public rhetoric in his well-known encomium for the Spartans dead at Thermopylai. Visibility and invisibility are a factor in the poem from the outset, if

---

τονος [or "backward turning," reading παλίντροπος]) harmony as of a bow or a lyre" (fr. B51 VS), says Heraklitos, apparently describing both the syntax of human life and the method of his own sentences. G. S. Kirk explains the Heraklitean bow as "a connexion working in both directions . . . which operates simultaneously in contrary ways and is only maintained so long as each tension exactly balances the other": (1954), 203. There is no ancient gossip associating the two thinkers, and I do not mean to imply that Simonides studied Heraklitos, yet one cannot but be struck by similarities of metaphysic and of technique. Cf. note 20 above, and see further below.

[29] Sullivan (1980), 33.

[30] Rosenmeyer (1965), 229. On the Heraklitean sentence, see further Hoffman (1925); Robinson (1987), 261; Snell (1926), 368–70.

Herodotos is correct that no corpses were recovered to Sparta from Thermopylai after the incident.[31] This is a dirge performed at an empty tomb. Its words bring the tombless bodies at Thermopylai and the bodiless tomb at Sparta into living relation:

τῶν ἐν Θερμοπύλαις θανόντων
εὐκλεὴς μὲν ἁ τύχα, καλὸς δ' ὁ πότμος,
βωμὸς δ' ὁ τάφος, πρὸ γόων δὲ μνᾶστις, ὁ δ' οἶκτος ἔπαινος·
ἐντάφιον δὲ τοιοῦτον εὐρὼς
οὔθ' ὁ πανδαμάτωρ ἀμαυρώσει χρόνος.
ανδρῶν ἀγαθῶν ὅδε σηκὸς οἰκέταν εὐδοξίαν
Ἑλλάδος εἵλετο· μαρτυρεῖ δὲ καὶ Λεωνίδας,
Σπάρτας βασιλεύς, ἀρετᾶς μέγαν λελοιπὼς
κόσμον ἀέναόν τε κλέος.[32]

[Of those dead in Thermopylai
glorious is the misfortune, good the doom,
the grave is an altar, in place of laments
is memory, the grief is praise.
Such an epitaph as this neither rust
nor all-annihilating time will darken.
This tomb of good men has chosen
the glory of Greece as its inhabitant.
And in fact Leonidas himself is witness,
king of Sparta: he left
excellence as a mark of beauty,
he left glory flowing forever.]

The poem begins with five statements that compose a fivefold conceptual shock (vv. 2–3). Simonides lines up a series of nouns and adjectives in tensile pairs, so that they seem to defy one another and to threaten the conventional categories of epitaphic diction:

Glorious the misfortune, good the doom,
an altar the grave, for groanings memory,
    the grief praise.

[31] Herodotos 7.228.
[32] Simonides fr. 531 *PMG*.

There are five sentences here, yet no verb can be seen. Simonides creates a syntax of defiance out of simple apposition, as a painter may set daubs of pure color next to each other on his canvas in the knowledge that they will mix on the retina of your eye.[33] The aligned words do not refute or replace one another, they interdepend; the meaning of the sentences happens not outside, not inside the daubs of paint, but *between* them:

> The grave is an altar. . . .

Neither grave nor altar could be what it is—mean what it means—without the other.[34] Visible and invisible lock together in a fact composed of their difference. At the edge where they meet, an area of very bright light is generated and out of the light steps Leonidas (v. 7) as witness of his own fame—"Not perfectly logically," says Hermann Fränkel in his commentary on this poem, "for the general statement is proved by a reversion to the previous topic as an illustration."[35] Leonidas, then, embodies the not-perfect logic of the whole poem. He stands in apposition to himself. Living and dead at the same time, Leonidas is his own exemplum, an invisible manifestation of the fact that the standard categories into which logic would divide the world are nowhere truly separable. His immortal mortality is a single fact seen from two vanishing points at once, in defiance of the laws of painterly perspective.

The verbal techniques of ἀπάτη with which Simonides conjures Leonidas from death in this poem might well have impressed a Protagoras or a Gorgias.[36] But we can distinguish the poet's intention from the sophists' in important ways. Gorgias tells us that reality, if it exists at all, is incommunicable and that the function

---

[33] Cf. Plato *Crito* 107d. That this phenomenon was known to ancient painters under the name σκιαγραφία is the hypothesis of Keuls (1975); (1978), 60–61.

[34] With this notably relational conception of how language operates we might compare the attitude of the historical Simonides to slander. Stobaios records that, when a friend told Simonides that he was hearing much bad talk about him, the poet replied, "Will you not stop defaming me with your ears!" (2.42).

[35] Fränkel (1973), 320.

[36] Cf., e.g., Gorgias fr. B82.13 *VS*.

of words is to create an autonomous reality serving the rhetorical needs of the moment.[37] Gorgias honors λόγος for its detachment from things and, at the same time, its wily power to dissemble attachment. Simonides, on the other hand, holds λόγος to be εἰκὼν τῶν πραγμάτων, a picture of things; he is not inclined to regard reality as a function of his art nor his art as a manipulation of surfaces. When Simonides composes a poem like his encomium for Leonidas, with its clean machinery of appositions, vanishing points and conceptual shocks, his motive is not rhetorical. He is painting a picture of things that brings visible and invisible together in the mind's eye as one coherent fact. The coherence is a poetic conjuring, but the fact is not. Together they generate a surplus value that guarantees poetic vocation against epistemological stinginess. To make "paintings that talk" is to engage in a conversation that is more than words and beyond price.

SLEEP

Let us study Simonidean iconology in another, more colorful painting, the famous Danaë fragment. The poem tells the story of Danaë and her infant son Perseus, put to sea in a box because of a sinister prophecy:

>   ὅτε λάρνακι
> ἐν δαιδαλέαι
> ἄνεμός τέ μιν πνέων
> κινηθεῖσά τε λίμνα δείματι
> ἔρειπεν, οὐκ ἀδιάντοισι παρειαῖς
> αμφί τε Περσέι βάλλε φίλαν χέρα
> εἶπέν τ'· ὦ τέκος, οἷον ἔχω πόνον·
>
> σὺ δ' ἀωτεῖς, γαλαθηνῶι
> δ' ἤτορι κνοώσσεις
> ἐν ἀτερπέι δούρατι χαλκεογόμφωι
> νυκτί τ' ἀλαμπέι
> κυανέωι τε δνόφωι σταλείς·

---

[37] Frr. B3, B82.8 *VS.*

ἄχναν δ᾽ ὕπερθε τεᾶν κομᾶν
βαθεῖαν παριόντος
κύματος οὐκ ἀλέγεις, οὐδ᾽ ἀνέμου
φθόγγον, πορφυρέαι
κείμενος ἐν χλανίδι, πρόσωπον καλόν.
εἰ δέ τοι δεινὸν τό γε δεινὸν ἦν,
καί κεν ἐμῶν ῥημάτων
λεπτὸν ὑπεῖχες οὖας.

κέλομαι δ᾽, εὗδε βρέφος,
εὑδέτω δὲ πόντος, εὑδέτω δ᾽ ἄμετρον κακόν·
μεταβουλία δέ τις φανείη,
Ζεῦ πάτερ, ἐκ σέο·
ὅττι δὲ θαρσαλέον ἔπος εὔχομαι
ἢ νόσφι δίκας,
σύγγνωθί μοι.[38]

[. . . When
in the painted box—
wind blasting her,
waves going wild,
knocked flat by fear,
her face streaming water,
she put her hand around Perseus and said,
"O child, what trouble I have!
Yet you sleep on soundly,
deep in infant's dreams
in this bleak box of wood,
nailed together, nightflashing,
in the blue blackness you lie
stretched out.
Waves tower over your head,
water rolls past—you pay no attention at all,
don't hear the shriek of the wind,
you just lie still in your bright blanket,
beautiful face.

[38] Simonides fr. 543 *PMG*.

But if to you the terrible were terrible,
you would lend your small ear
to what I am saying.
Ah now, little one, I bid you sleep.
Let the sea sleep,
let the immeasurable evil sleep.
And I pray some difference may come to light
father Zeus, from you!
Yet if my prayer is rude
or outside justice,
forgive me."]

Throughout the poem Danaë is awake, terrified and talking; the baby is silently, serenely asleep. Simonides has chosen to construct the poem as an alignment of two consciousnesses: one of them is present, active and accessible to us, the other has vanished inwardly.[39] One of them is cognizant of the reality that we see stretched out around it, the other is oblivious of that reality and apparently paying attention to something quite different behind its closed eyes.

The difference between their two states of mind is the chief subject of Danaë's discourse, addressed to the baby (vv. 7–21) as the sea rises around them. Placed exactly at the center of her utterance and her emotion is a contrafactual sentence (vv. 18–20) that operates like a vanishing point for these two perspectives on reality:

But if to you the terrible were terrible
you would lend your small ear
to what I am saying.

In its perfect symmetry, the protasis (εἰ δέ τοι δεινὸν τὸ γε δεινὸν ἦν) is a picture of the cognitive dissonance that obtains between these two states of mind. The world of Danaë and the world of

---

[39] Perhaps Simonides' acclaimed ability to arouse τὸ σύμπαθες (*Vita Aeschyli* 8; Dionysios of Halikarnassos *De oratoribus veteribus* 420 Reiske; Quintilian *Institutio oratoria* 10.1.64) can be understood as a similar action of alignment that, by positioning one πάθος alongside (συν) another, discovers sympathy between them. Insofar as λόγος is εἰκών, he paints an etymology of emotion.

Perseus are set alongside one another as two different perceptions of the same physical situation, two discrepant definitions of the same word, τὸ δεινὸν, "the terrible." It is strange to think how such divergence is possible. Where does the baby's mind go when he is lost in sleep? To judge from his untroubled demeanor, he has gone somewhere more pleasant than the wild sea where his mother is pitching and tossing. Perhaps, as Heraklitos says, "the invisible harmony is better than the visible one,"[40] but we do not know that. What we do know, as we stare at this painting, is that Perseus' state of mind is something as real as his mother's state of mind, although different and inaccessible. Neither consciousness refutes or replaces the other: they interdepend. They are reciprocally invisible. In Heraklitos' words, "Men asleep are laborers and coworkers of what is going on in this world."[41]

The meaning of Simonides' poem is something that happens *between* the two worlds of waking and sleeping. At vv. 21–22 Danaë repeats the same verb three times: "I bid you, sleep, little one, let the sea sleep, let the immeasurable evil sleep" (v. 22). The next verse is a prayer (μεταβουλία δέ τις φανείη, "I pray some difference may come to light," 23) and out of the prayer steps father Zeus ("Father Zeus, from you," 24). When Danaë modulates from the second person imperative εὖδε ("sleep, little one") in v. 21 to the third person imperative εὑδέτω ("let the sea sleep") in v. 22, she moves from a literal to a figurative register of speech and conjures up the differentiating power of God. Poetic language has this capacity to uncover a world of metaphor that lies inside all our ordinary speech like a mind asleep. *If to you the terrible were terrible,*" says Danaë to her sleeping child, "you would hear what I am saying." But the child does not hear and a different kind of sleeping has to be imagined by the wakeful mother. "*If to you the invisible were visible,*" says Simonides to his audience, "you would see God." But we do not see God and a different kind of visibility has to be created by the watchful poet. The poet's metaphorical activity puts him in a contrafactual relation to the world of other

[40] Fr. B54 *VS.*
[41] Fr. B75 *VS.*

people and ordinary speech. He does not seek to refute or re-
place that world but merely to indicate its lacunae, by positioning
alongside the world of things that we see an uncanny protasis of
things invisible, although no less real. Without poetry these two
worlds would remain unconscious of one another. As Heraklitos
says, "All we see awake is death, all we see asleep is sleep."[42] At the
vanishing point of metaphor we may catch a glimpse of their
differentiation.

To problematize the relation between the worlds of waking and
sleeping was a poetic strategy that occurred to Simonides more
than once, and fascinated him even outside poetic practice. Xen-
ophon records a dialogue between Simonides and Hieron, tyrant
of Syracuse, in which they analyze various gradations of pleasure
and perception in sleep states and nonsleep states.[43] Somewhat
more cryptic is a passage from the elegiac corpus of Theognis
where Simonides is admonished:

Do not wake one who is sleeping, Simonides,
one whom sweet sleep seizes when he is drunk with wine,
nor bid the wakeful one against his will to go to sleep.

Interpretation of these Theognidean verses remains controversial
and it is tempting to dismiss the passage as symposiastic cliché,[44]
but perhaps there is more here than meets the eye. We might
again compare Simonides' thought with Heraklitean usage,
where wakefulness is a metaphor for the philosopher's epistemic
distance from a world of sleepwalkers.[45] These sleepers are the
generality of men, who fail to make sense of their experience and
live at odds with their own life, lost in what Heraklitos calls "idiot
thinking" (ἴδια φρόνησις).[46] Idiot thinking is a matter of mistak-
ing the visible surface of things, the world of appearance and
seeming, for the true, underlying, nonapparent λόγος that Hera-

[42] Fr. B21 *VS.*

[43] Xenophon *Hieron* 1.6.

[44] Theognis 469–71. Carrière does not address vv. 469–71 separately but al-
ludes to the preceding verses as "précepte de l'hospitalité antique": (1962), 49.

[45] Cf. Heraklitos frr. B1, 21, 26, 71, 75, 88, 89 *VS;* Kahn (1979), 99, 213–16,
255, 294; Marcovich (1967), 10, 245; Fink and Heidegger (1979).

[46] Fr. B2 *VS.*

klitos calls "invisible harmony."[47] In Simonides too we have noticed an attunement to the invisible harmony of things. His poems are paintings of a counterworld that lies behind the facts and inside perceived appearances. There is one striking fragment in which Simonides confesses his commitment to it:

τὸ δοκεῖν καὶ τὰν ἀλάθειαν βιᾶται.[48]

which means something like,

Appearance constrains even truth.

Or we could overtranslate it:

It is in fact upon the world of things needing to be uncovered that the world of merely visible things keeps exerting its pressure.

SEE NOT

Simonides spent his literary as well as his historical life exerting a counterpressure to the claims of the merely visible world. The project is an iconology informing his verse. But a poet's life is a kind of icon too. When we look more closely at the daubs of paint that compose Simonides' traditional biography, it is interesting to see, there too, visibles and invisibles in tension or transformation, as if the poet had mixed the colors himself. We have already heard the story of his mnemonic system, whose invention was due to the sudden vanishing of a roomful of people and whose technique was one of visualizing data as faces around a dinner table. We have heard how Simonides kept two large boxes at home: one for visible, the other for invisible χάρις.[49] It is also recorded that he added a third string to the lyre, devised four new letters for the

[47] Fr. B54; cf. B56 *VS*.

[48] Simonides fr. 598 *PMG*. The sentence is cited without attribution by Plato (*Republic* 364) as if it constituted an argument for specious virtue. In the absence of any original context for the fragment, it is hard to know how tendentious Plato's reading is. On Simonides misrepresented by Plato, see Bell (1978), 77–81; Woodbury (1953).

[49] See above. Scholia *ad* Theokritos 16; Stobaios 3.10.39; Plutarch *Moralia* 520a.

Greek alphabet and when asked why he had composed an inscription for the paintings of Polygnotos at Delphi, replied, "So that it might be conspicuous that Polygnotos had painted them."[50] There is also a fable told by Phaedrus, about how Simonides was once a victim of shipwreck. As the other passengers scurried about the sinking ship trying to save their possessions, the poet stood idle. When questioned, he declared, "Mecum mea sunt cuncta": "Everything that *is* me is *with* me."

Finally, God. One day in Syrakuse the tyrant Hieron asked Simonides to define the nature and attributes of divinity. Had the sophist Protagoras been around to hear this question he would have said, "As a matter of fact, nothing can be known about God." Protagoras would have given two reasons why we cannot know God: namely, the shortness of human life and the invisibility of the subject matter.[51] But Simonides was not so sure. "Give me a day to think about it," said Simonides to Hieron. After a day Hieron repeated his question. "Give me two days to think about it," said Simonides to Hieron. Two days later Hieron asked again. "Give me four days to think about it," said Simonides, and so it continued, exponentially, until at last Hieron demanded an explanation. Whereupon Simonides said, "The longer I ponder the matter, the more obscure it seems to me."[52]

Simonides has bequeathed to us in this anecdote a sort of concrete poem of man's relations with the Godhead. And what we see enacted in the interchange with Hieron is the properly invisible nature of divinity, receding out of our grasp down the lengthening corridor of time and into the darkness at the back of the painting. No trick of perspective, no illusionist sleight-of-hand, can bring God into focus on this canvas.[53] Simonides is interested in rendering the fact that ἀλάθεια (truth) cannot be seen in this world, no matter how tyrannical the pressure exerted on it by τὸ δοκεῖν

[50] Plutarch *Moralia* 438b.

[51] Cf. fr. B4 *VS*.

[52] "Quia quanto diutius considero tanto mihi res videtur obscurior": Cicero *De natura deorum* 1.22.

[53] Cf. Heraklitos: "Nature loves to hide itself" (φύσις κρυπτέσθαι φιλεῖ B123 *VS*).

(appearances). The painting he creates is not one that would please a Zeuxis or a Protagoras. Here is a difference of bone structure, not just technique.[54] Like the sophist, the illusionist painter defines the world as data and undertakes to enhance our experience of it by perfecting our control of it. He claims to make his audience see, as it were, what is not there. Simonides' claim is more radical, for it comprehends the profoundest of poetic experiences: that of *not* seeing what *is* there.

CELAN

In a curious piece of prose called *Conversation in the Mountains*,[55] Celan speaks of visibles, invisibles, alienation, God and sleep. This text invites comparison with Simonides' whole way of thinking about these matters, but especially with his Danaë poem (fr. 543). Both Celan's *Conversation in the Mountains* and Simonides' Danaë poem are works of indeterminate genre. The Danaë fragment is called a dithyramb by some and a dirge by others. No one is sure of its scansion, colometry or occasion; we owe its preservation to Dionysios of Halikarnassos, who quoted the text without line breaks in order to show that if poetry were written out as prose you couldn't tell the difference.[56] Celan's *Conversation in the Mountains,* partly based on Büchner's novella *Lenz* (as well as on works by Kafka, Buber and Mandelstam), reads like something between a parable and a screenplay. In places its incantatory prose resembles a prayer or a lullaby. Moreover, like Simonides' poem, Celan's tale uses sleep as an image of differentiation. For it is the story of a person named Klein who is as lonely as Danaë and longs for conversation, but finds himself facing a world that does not hear him. It is a world "folded over on itself, once and twice and three times." Klein describes it also as a world of sleepers:

[54] "If you call painting mute poetry, you might as well call poetry blind painting," Leonardo says tartly in his *Treatise;* McMahon (1956), 29; Markiewicz (1987), 338.

[55] Celan (1990), 23–29; Felstiner (1995), 141–44; Waldrop (1986), 17–22.

[56] Dionysios of Halikarnassos *De compositione verborum* 26.

Auf dem Stein bin ich gelegen, damals, du weißt, auf den Steinfliesen; und neben mir, da sind sie gelegen, die andern, die wie ich waren, die andern, die anders waren als ich und genauso, die Geschwisterkinder; und sie lagen da und schliefen, schliefen und schliefen nicht, und sie träumten und träumten nicht, und sie liebten mich nicht und ich liebte sie nicht. . . .

[On the stone is where I lay, back then you know, on the stone slabs; and next to me they were lying there, the others, who were like me, the others, who were different from me and just the same, the kinsmen; and they lay there and slept, slept and did not sleep, and they dreamt and did not dream, and they did not love me and I did not love them. . . .]

Celan's tale tells of Klein taking an evening walk up into the mountains, where he meets his kinsman Gross and attempts to have a conversation. For, like Danaë, neither Klein nor Gross is at home in the silence of nature:

Still wars also, still dort oben im Gebirg. Nicht lang wars still, denn wenn der Jud daherkommt und begegnet einem zweiten, dann ists bald vorbei mit dem Schweigen, auch im Gebirg. Denn der Jud und die Natur, das ist zweierlei, immer noch, auch heute, auch hier.

[So it was quiet, quiet, up there in the mountains. It wasn't quiet for long because when one Jew comes along and meets another, then goodbye silence even in the mounains. Because the Jew and nature, that's two very different things, as always, even today, even here.]

Klein goes on to describe a landscape as impressive as the wild sea where Danaë is stranded:

Es hat sich die Erde gefaltet hier oben, hat sich gefaltet einmal und zweimal und dreimal, und hat sich aufgetan in der Mitte, und in der Mitte steht ein Wasser, und das Wasser ist grün, und das Grüne ist weiß, und das Weiße kommt von noch weiter oben, kommt von den Gletschern. . . .

[Up here the earth has folded over, it's folded once and twice and three times, and opened up in the middle, and in the middle there's

63

some water, and the water is green, and the green is white, and the white comes from up further, comes from the glaciers. . . .]

Celan tells us this landscape is both visible and invisible to Klein. For although Klein "has eyes," he is separated by "a movable veil" from what is going on in nature, so that everything he sees is "half image and half veil" (*halb Bild und halb Schleier*). Behind the veil, behind the folded-over surfaces of glaciers, behind the closed eyes of sleepers, lies something Klein cannot see or speak to. Klein feels his separation from the world behind the veil mainly as an incapacity of language:

> Das ist die Sprache, die hier gilt, das Grüne mit dem Weißen drin, eine Sprache, nicht für dich und nicht für mich—denn, frag ich, für wen ist sie denn gedacht, die Erde, nicht für dich, sag ich, ist sie gedacht, und nicht für mich—eine Sprache, je nun, ohne Ich und ohne Du, lauter Er, lauter Es, verstehst du, lauter Sie, und nichts als das.

> [That's the kind of speech that counts here, the green with the white in it, a language not for you and not for me—because I'm asking, who is it meant for then, the earth, it's not meant for you, I'm saying, and not for me—well then, a language with no I and no Thou, pure He, pure It, you see, pure She and nothing but that.]

Language is at issue because conversation, even amid the brutal snags to conversation that both Klein and Danaë experience, is the event that Celan and Simonides want to stage. Why has Klein come up into the mountains? "Because I had to talk, to myself or to you." What does Danaë beg of her sleeping child? "That you lend your small ear to what I am saying" (19–20). Neither of them finds their way to a satisfactory conversation but both insist on standing in the gap where it should take place, pointing to the lacunae where it burned. No more than Danaë is Klein able to find "speech that counts here." He cannot talk the language of glaciers, as she cannot speak to sleep or sea. Yet in the absence of a "language with no I and no Thou," Klein does manage to exchange some "babble" (*Geschwätz*) with his kinsman Gross. What kind of language is this?

The word *Geschwätz* is a common German term for everyday chitchat. But Felstiner suggests it may have for Celan "hints of Babel and the loss of original language." He explains:

> For in Walter Benjamin's essay "On Language in General and on the Language of Man," *Geschwätz* designates empty speech after the Fall, speech without Adam's power of naming. . . . The babbling of Celan's Jews is a comedown—via the cataclysm that ruined Benjamin—from God-given speech.[57]

Simonides also dramatizes the problem of naming. As Danaë struggles to find a name for something she knows as τὸ δεινόν ("the terrible"), she produces an anguished tautology ("If to you the terrible were terrible . . .") in which the two possibilities of babble and God-given speech stand side by side—the latter hauntingly translated into the former, as it must be here among *die Geschwätzigen.* We have no other words to use. We know they don't count but we lay them against the abyss anyway because they are what mark it for us, contrafactually. "There may be, in one direction, two kinds of strangeness next to each other," said Celan once.[58] So we see Danaë and her sleeping child aligned in a moment of reciprocal invisibility. Two kinds of strangeness may interdepend, marking the place where babble replaces speech that counts: the green with the white in it. Celan's tale sends Klein up into the mountains to confront this lacuna, which Celan names *Leerstelle* ("vacant space" or "empty place"):

> Da stehn sie, die Geschwisterkinder, auf einer Straße stehn sie im Gebirg, es schweigt der Stock, es schweigt der Stein, und das Schwei-gen ist kein Schweigen, kein Wort ist da verstummt und kein Satz, eine Pause ists bloß, eine Wortlücke ists, eine Leerstelle ists, du siehst alle Silben umherstehn; Zunge sind sie und Mund, diese beiden, wie zuvor, und in den Augen hängt ihnen der Schleier. . . . Die Geschwät-zigen!

[There the kinsmen (Klein and Gross) stand, standing on a road in

[57] Felstiner (1995), 145.

[58] Speech on the occasion of receiving the Georg Büchner Prize, Darmstadt, 22 October 1960: "The Meridian": Celan (1990), 40–62; Waldrop (1986), 37–55.

the mountains, the stick is silent, the stone is silent, and the silence is no silence, no word is going mute and no phrase, it's merely a pause, it's a word-gap, it's a vacant space, you can see the syllables all standing around; tongue is what they are and mouth, these two, like before, and the veil is hanging in their eyes. . . . The babblers!]

The *Leerstelle* with "syllables all standing around" is an eerie place and has the same effect on Klein as the wild waves do on Danaë. Both of them begin babbling into the void. And then, unexpectedly, stumble up against something else. Not the words they were seeking as a way to penetrate sleep, sea and glacier. Not the listener who will give ear to their words. But something else— something to which (I think) Celan alludes in his "Meridian" speech:

Das ist ein Hinaustreten aus dem Menschlichen, ein Sichhinaus-begeben in einen dem Meschlichen zugewandten und unheimlichen Bereich—denselben, in dem die Affengestalt, die Automaten und damit . . . ach, auch die Kunst zuhause zu sein scheinen.[59]

[This means going beyond what is human, stepping into a realm that is turned toward the human, but uncanny—the realm where the monkey, the automatons and with them . . . oh, art too, seem to be at home.]

Both Klein and Danaë address themselves to this uncanny realm and receive no answer at first. "Whoever speaks . . . no one hears him," says Klein in some despair. But then into the stupendous unlistening void, Klein and Danaë each hurl an act of strangeness of their own—a poetic act. Danaë flips the verb "sleep" open on a metaphor, leaving behind the literal sleep of her child that she cannot penetrate and moving instead to the register of analogy where all is possible and prayer begins:

> κέλομαι δ᾽, εὗδε βρέφος,
> εὑδέτω δὲ πόντος, εὑδέτω δ᾽ ἄμετρον κακόν.
> μεταβουλία δέ τις φανείη,
> Ζεῦ πάτερ, ἐκ σέο.

[59] Celan (1990), 47; Waldrop (1986), 42–43.

[Ah now, little one, I bid you sleep.

Let the sea sleep,

let the immeasurable evil sleep.

And I pray some difference may come to light,

father Zeus, from you!]

Klein, in an equally bold linguistic move, wrests the name of God out of his own post-Adamic babble. The phrase *hörst du* ("do you hear?"), recurrent in his stuttering exchange with Gross, suddenly takes on a capital letter and rises into Being as *Hörstdu* (Hearest Thou):

> Sagt er, sagt er. . . . Hörst du, sagt er. . . . Und Hörstdu, gewiß, Hörstdu, der sagt nichts, der antwortet nicht, denn Hörstdu, das ist der mit den Gletschern, der, der sich gefaltet hat, dreimal, und nicht für die Menschen.[60]

> [Says he, says he. . . . Do you hear, he says. . . . And Hearest Thou, of course, Hearest Thou, he says nothing, he doesn't answer, because Hearest Thou, that's the one with the glaciers, the one who folded himself over, three times, and not for humans.]

Hörstdu does not respond to Klein's feat of naming, any more than Zeus answers Danaë's prayer, but still: the movable veil has moved. Spirit is named in an empty place. It is worth noting that about the time he was writing "Conversation," Celan bought a book on Martin Buber and underlined the sentences:

> Creatures stand within the secret of Creation, of Speech . . . we can say thou because thou is also said to us. . . . Spirit is not in the I but between I and Thou.[61]

When he aligns "the secret of Creation" with the secret "of Speech," Buber makes a theoretical point about Spirit that Celan and Simonides prefer to stage as conversation. The point is twofold. For, on the one hand, Spirit does not come from somewhere

---

[60] Celan (1990), 26; Waldrop (1986), 20.

[61] Concerning the influence of Buber's "Gespräch in den Bergen" (1913) on Celan's "Gespräch im Gebirg" (1960), see Felstiner (1995), 140–44; and Lyon (1971), 110–20.

else, it is already present—invisible—within the elements of speech here in use. At the same time, Spirit does not arise of its own accord, but is wrested from behind the veil by an effort of language between I and Thou. The effort, as Simondes and Celan stage it, is very like a poetic act: reaching right to the edge of ordinary babble, to the place where metaphor waits and naming occurs. This is the act that Simonides calls λὸγος and defines as "a picture of things," for it contains visibles and invisibles side by side, strangeness by strangeness. It is a word of perfect and radical mimetic economy. From such a word, as Danaë hopes (and the poets confirm), "difference may come to light."

EN ROUTE

A kind of peace seems to be settling over the end of Simonides' poem when Danaë repeats the word "sleep" three times as if she were beginning a lullaby. Near the end of Celan's tale, too, comes a seemingly peaceful allusion, to a "candle burning down," perhaps a Sabbatic candle.[62] What cause for peace? I suppose we could say glaciers, sleep and sea have been confronted; the terrible has (according to our lights) been named; Spirit moved in a place between. Yet neither Simonides nor Celan allows himself to end in peace and Spirit. Both texts recoil on a hard blast of self. Compare Danaë's final apotropaic cry ("Yet if my prayer is rude or outside justice, forgive me!") with the last words of Jew Klein:

> —Ich hier, ich; ich, der ich dir all das sagen kann, sagen hätt können; der ich dirs nicht sag und nicht gesagt hab; ich mit dem Türkenbund links, ich mit der Rapunzel, ich mit der heruntergebrannten, der Kerze, ich mit dem Tag, ich mit den Tagen, ich hier und ich dort, ich, begletitet vielleicht—jetzt!—von der Liebe der Nichtgeliebten, ich auf dem Weg hier zu mir, oben.

> [—I here, I; I, who can say, could have said, all that to you; who don't say and haven't said it to you; I with the Turk's-cap on the left, I with

---

[62] Celan describes a candle lit by "our mother's father"; Felstiner reads it as an image of candles lit by a mother to mark the end of one week and the beginning of the next: (1995), 145.

the Rampion, I with what burned down, the candle, I with the day, I
with the days, I here and I there, I, companioned perhaps—now!—by
the love of those not loved, I on the way to myself, up there.]

Klein is a survivor—small, scrappy, bereft, but awake and en
route. Like Danaë, Klein holds his ground in a final gesture of
radical individuation. The stubborn loneliness of this scenario
seems drawn from a certain conception of the poetic calling that
(I think) would have made sense to Simonides, and that Celan
describes in the Meridian speech:

Das Gedicht behauptet sich am Rande seiner selbst. . . . Das Gedicht
ist einsam. Es ist einsam und unterwegs. Wer es schreibt, bleibt ihm
mitgegeben.[63]

[The poem holds its ground on its own margin. . . . The poem is
lonely. It is lonely and en route. Its author stays with it.]

When I reread Simonides' Danaë fragment with these sen-
tences of Celan in mind, the poem makes sense to me as a picture
of the poet's situation: her loneliness, her marginality, her sense
of the relation between visibles and invisibles, her staying power—
through catastrophe to metaphor, to naming, to prayer. And yes,
her utter wakefulness. Before closing the discussion of Danaë, let
us consider one more poem in which Celan chooses imagery of
wakefulness and sleep. Because I think this is a poem about the
poet's effort, so beautifully painted for us by Simonides, to "stay
with" the poem:

[ALLE DIE SCHLAFGESTALTEN, kristallin,
die du annahmst
im Sprachschatten,

ihnen
führ ich mein Blut zu,

die Bildzeilen, sie
soll ich bergen

---

[63] Celan (1990), 55; Waldrop (1986), 49.

in den Schlitzvenen
meiner Erkenntnis—,

meine Trauer, ich seh's,
läuft zu dir über.[64]

ALL THOSE SLEEP SHAPES, crystalline,
that you assumed
in the language shadow,

to those
I lead my blood,

those image lines, them
I'm to harbor
in the slit-arteries
of my cognition—,

my grief, I can see,
is deserting to you.]

Perhaps because he is awake among the sleepers, Celan begins on the dark side of words "in the language shadow." Here he sees shapes that belong to "sleep" and to "you," which he approaches. They are "crystalline" shapes—interior and elemental designs— which the poet will capture in a picture form or outlines (*Bild-zeilen*) and store in his blood. Blood is also the place where a poet's understanding takes place (*Erkenntnis*). To understand and to keep, in however diminished a form, some picture of the inside crystal of things—perhaps what Klein calls "the green with the white in it"—is a poet's obligation (*soll ich*) and places him in a certain relation of "I" to "you." Whoever "you" are, you are placed at the beginning and end of the poem, to enclose the poet in the middle and make his existence possible for him in two essential ways: for you take on shapes that he can understand and you give him a place for his grief.

The poem ends in this place of grief, on an unlikely verb. "My grief, I can see, is deserting to you." The verb *überlaufen* means "to

[64] Celan (1983), 3:79; (1988), 336–37.

well up and run over" (as milk boiling on the stove) or "to rise up and run across" (as desertion). Both its domestic and its military connotations convey an action of displacement—here to there, mine to you—and a mood of error—milk that boils over is lost or spoilt, desertion is a punishable offense. But if these verses do in some part concern the mysterious encounter of I and Thou that gives rise to a poem, why do they choose to represent encounter as transgression or excess, as overflow and misdemeanor? For after all, it is Celan's stated view that the inception of a poem relies entirely upon this encounter (or the effort toward it). So he says in the Meridian speech:

> Das Gedicht will zu einem Andern, es braucht dieses Andere, es braucht ein Gegenüber. Es sucht es auf, es spricht sich ihm zu. Jedes Ding, jeder Mensch ist dem Gedicht, das auf das Andere zuhält, eine Gestalt dieses Anderen.[65]

> [The poem intends another, needs this other, needs an opposite. It goes toward it, bespeaks it. For the poem, everything and everybody is a figure of this other toward which it is heading.]

Celan sees the poem as heading toward an "other" and the poet as bent on this encounter. He describes the poet's method (a bit later in the Meridian speech) with the word "attention" (*Aufmerksamkeit*) and defines attention as "the natural prayer of the soul."[66] Let us permit prayer to return us to the analogy with Simonides' Danaë. Her conversation with an "other," which shifts its focus from sleeping child to angry sea to Zeus, also ends in prayer. Her prayer, moreover, combines an action of displacement and a mood of error. For she suddenly sees herself "rude and outside justice" and appeals for forgiveness. It is hard to see what excess or transgression she fears to have committed. Could Zeus possibly blame her pain or fault her cry for help? But that is the point. In encounters with Thou, you never know. Who can read the mind of Zeus? It is turned away. The properly invisible

---

[65] Celan (1990), 55; Waldrop (1986), 49.

[66] "If you allow me a quote from Malebranche via Walter Benjamin's essay on Kafka": Celan (1990), 56; Waldrop (1986), 50.

nature of otherness guarantees the mystery of our encounters with it, pulls out of us the act of attention that may bring "some difference" to light here. Danaë prays for difference—we all do— without knowing what is entailed in that. When our grief deserts us, where does it go and who will we be without it? These are questions that remain in the empty place where ἀλάθεια (truth) and τὸ δοκεῖν (appearances) lie side by side, strangeness by strangeness, exerting on one another a terrible and sleepless pressure that only the poet attends.

CHAPTER III

Epitaphs

SIMONIDES

No genre of verse is more profoundly concerned with seeing what is not there, and not seeing what is, than that of the epitaph. An epitaph is something placed upon a grave—a σῶμα that becomes a σῆμα, a body that is made into a sign. Already in Homer there is mention of a σῆμα or tomb heaped up high over a dead warrior so that some passerby in later time will stop and remark on it.[1] The purpose of the monument is to insert a dead and vanished past into the living present. Not until the seventh century B. C. did this insertion become an inscribed event; not until the lifetime of Simonides of Keos did the inscription fall into the hands of a master poet and become a major art form.

Simonides was the most prolific composer of epitaphs in the ancient world and set the conventions of the genre. The formal sale of pity contributed substantially to his fortune and became inseparable from his name. We find "tears of Simonides" (*lacrimis Simonideis*) used as a byword for poetry of lament by the Roman poet Catullus. We hear ancient scholiasts commending the special qualities of "sympathy" and "pathos" that distinguish Simonidean verse.[2] What did they get for their money, the mourners who bought tears from Simonides?

EXCHANGE

A salesman of memorial verse has to think very closely about the relation, measurable in cash, between letter shapes cut on a stone

---

[1] Homer *Iliad* 7.81–91; Raubitschek (1968), 5–7.

[2] Catullus 38.7; τὸ συμπαθές: *Vita Aeschyli* 119, cf. Dionysios of Halikarnassos *De imitatione* 2.420; Horace *Carmina* 2.1.37–40; Quintilian *Institutio oratoria* 10.1.64.

and the condition of timeless attention that the Greeks call memory. Simonides was struck by the implications of this task, as various anecdotes from his traditional biography attest. Remember his adventure with a corpse on a beach. This story instantiates the epitaphic contract: a poet is someone who saves and is saved by the dead. And although the anecdote is likely apocryphal, its metaphysic can be felt throughout his poetry (and in graveside rhetoric down to the present day).[3] What Simonides contributed to our style of thinking and talking about death is a central shaping metaphor: the metaphor of exchange. Here is an example of his epitaphic work:

ἡγεμόνεσσι δὲ μισθὸν Ἀθηναῖοι τάδ' ἔδωκαν
    ἀντ' εὐεργεσίης καὶ μεγάλων ἀγαθῶν·
μᾶλλόν τις τάδ' ἰδὼν καὶ ἐπεσσομένων ἐθελήσει
    ἀμφὶ περὶ ξυνοῖς πράγμασι δῆριν ἔχειν.[4]

[And to the leaders as a wage the Athenians gave this
    in exchange for service and great goods.
All the more will a man of the future (seeing this) choose
    to enter battle for the common benefit.]

This inscription was probably carved on a herm c. 475 B.C. to commemorate an Athenian victory against the Persians in Thrace.[5] Notice the figurative language Simonides has chosen here to represent the relation between death on the battlefield and life on a monument, between soldiers whose lives are past and citizens whose lives are still before them. It is a transactional relationship, as the noun μισθός ("wage") and the preposition ἀντί ("in exchange for") and the noun εὐεργεσία ("benefaction") imply. Money is not mentioned but we feel the presence of a metaphysical question of value. It is a question at least as old as Achilles, a question whose contours have been sharpened (I think) for Simonides and for his audience by personal experience of money transactions. "Money can exchange any quality or object

[3] Lattimore, (1962), 168–73.
[4] Simonides fr. 40[c] *FGE*.
[5] Jacoby (1945), 185ff.; Page (1981), 255–58; Wade-Gery (1933), 82ff.

for any other, even contradictory qualities and objects," says Marx.[6] Achilles would not have agreed. Achilles' answer to the question of value was simple: no object or quality in the world (he decided) was worth as much as his own breath of life. [7] Achilles put a veto on the heroic exchange of death for glory. But this exchange is absolutely fundamental to the politics of the public epitaph, as Simonides says bluntly in the last couplet of this poem:

> All the more will a man of the future (seeing this) choose
>   to enter battle for the common benefit.

A poet's task is to carry the transaction forward, from those who can no longer speak to those who may yet read (and must yet die).

The political terms of epitaphic transaction are set out also in Simonides' epitaph for men fallen in the battle of Euboea:

> Δίρφυος ἐδμήθημεν ὑπὸ πτυχί, σῆμα δ᾽ ἐφ᾽ ἡμῖν
>   ἐγγύθεν Εὐρίπου δημοσίαι κέχυται·
> οὐκ ἀδίκως, ἐρατὴν γὰρ ἀπωλέσαμεν νεότητα
>   τρηχεῖαν πολέμου δεξάμενοι νεφέλην.[8]

> [Underneath the fold of Dirphys we were broken, but a sign on top
>   of us
>   near Euripos at public expense has been heaped up—
> *not unjustly:* for we lost lovely youth
>   and took in exchange the jagged cloud of war.]

This poem measures out a system of exchanges, syntactic, spatial and moral. Dirphys (the mountain site of the battle) is set over against Euripos (the river site of the grave) as "underneath" is balanced by "on top of" and men laid low in the ground by a tomb rising above them. The men have made an explicit exchange of "lovely youth" for the "jagged cloud of war" and in this exchange is implied the contrast of "public expense" (which is named) with private cost (which is not), of visible "sign" (which we see) with buried signifier (which we do not).

---

[6] McLellan (1977), 111.
[7] Homer *Iliad* 9.401–11.
[8] Simonides fr. 2 *FGE*.

If Page is correct that this epigram commemorates the Euboeans (not the Athenians) who fell in the battle of Euboea,[9] it is a poem of uncommon candor. The Euboeans lost the battle of Euboea. Simonides states the fact baldly: "We were broken." Then adds an economic detail: "At public expense" a stone was raised. Why mention this? Certainly public payment indicates public honor. But it also raises the question of value, an awkward question for men who have lost a war. Simonides meets this question at the beginning of the third verse, with a blunt double-negative construction that confronts and denies all possibility of a bad exchange: "*not unjustly.*" The dead men rather jarringly assert that they were worth the price of their own tomb.

"To be exchanged, commodities must be somehow comparable," says Aristotle. "That is why money was invented. It provides a sort of mediator. For it measures all things, their relative value—for example, how many shoes are equal to a house, etc."[10] Or how many lines of elegiac verse are equal to an army of dead Euboeans. Emphasized by enjambement before and strong punctuation after, the phrase "not unjustly" could easily have been placed for irony or left open like a bad bargain. Instead these two words form the exact center of a moral and verbal equilibrium that imitates the process of exchange and justifies its own expenditure, like two beads of an abacus drawn together to mark the equity of profit and loss.

Consider now a slightly different example, where the facts of exchange touch Simonides personally. Of the three stones erected at Thermopylai to honor the men who fell with Leonidas, Simonides composed (probably all three but certainly) this one:

μνῆμα τόδε κλεινοῖο Μεγιστία, ὅν ποτε Μῆδοι
    Σπερχειὸν ποταμὸν κτεῖναν ἀμειψάμενοι,
μάντιος, ὅς ποτε Κῆρας ἐπερχομένας σάφα εἰδώς
    οὐκ ἔτλη Σπάρτης ἡγεμόνας προλιπεῖν.[11]

[9] Page (1981), 189–92.
[10] Aristotle *Nicomachean Ethics* 1133a19–23.
[11] Simonides fr. 6 *FGE.*

[Here is the tomb of glorious Megistias whom once on a day
   the Medes killed when they crossed Spercheios River.
Once on a day he saw Deaths coming at him
   but the leaders of Sparta he would not forsake.]

Megistias was a prophet, traveling with the Spartan army, who was
present at Thermopylai on the eve of the battle and foretold his
own death on the field. Although urged by the Spartan com-
mander to depart, he stayed and was killed the next day. We learn
from Herodotos that the erection of his tomb took place in some-
what unusual economic circumstances. For the other two monu-
ments at Thermopylai were set up at public expense by the Am-
phictyonic League, but the stone for Megistias was inscribed (that
is, paid for) by Simonides himself "because of a bond of guest-
friendship between the two of them" (κατὰ ξεινίην).[12] It is inter-
esting, then, that this poem, for which Simonides unusually re-
ceived no remuneration, makes use of the standard metaphors of
exchange in an unusual way.

Simonides highlights the concept of exchange by placing at the
center of the poem (at the end of v. 2) the resonant participle
ἀμειψάμενοι. This participle is from the verb ἀμείβομαι, which
means "to change" and can refer to change of position in space,
as when the Medes cross the Spercheios River, or to interchange
of question and answer, as when a prophet responds to inquiry, or
to exchange of goods or money in a commercial transaction. It is
a verb that can be active or passive, that can represent either or
both sides of an exchange. A particularly appropriate verb, then,
in a poem about a man who can see both sides of a river, a
prophet who can see both sides of a moment in time. This fatally
two-sided moment is isolated twice by Simonides with repetition
of the adverb ποτε ("once on a day"). Megistias is a prophet who
must both ask and answer the question of his own death, as Si-
monides must both buy and sell the poem that remembers him.
For a gravestone is a coin with more than two sides. Inscribed on
its surface are words that transform its commodity into communi-

12 Herodotos 7.228.

cation and project its usefulness across time. Aristotle defines money as "a guarantee of exchange in the future for something not given in the present."[13] So does the gravestone of Megistias guarantee a future exchange of oblivion for memory and purchase a moment of life for him each time its inscription is read.

Surface

Which brings us to reading and writing, and to a set of historical factors that may very concretely underlie Simonides' insight into the exchange of life and death that happens on a gravestone. Simonides' inscriptional verse is the first poetry in the ancient Greek tradition about which we can certainly say, these are texts written to be read: literature. Now it is true Simonidean diction contains frequent epicisms and his metrics depend upon Homer's; it is also likely that most people who read a Simonidean epitaph did so by sounding the words out loud.[14] Nonetheless, this is not oral verse in its composition nor in its aesthetic. The difference is physical: Simonides' poem has to fit on the stone bought for it. An oral poet may labor under restrictions of time or personal stamina or social decorum but only an inscriptional poet has to measure his inspiration against the size of his writing surface. Out of this material fact—which is also an economic fact because stones and stonecutting cost money—evolved an aesthetic of exactitude or verbal economy that became the hallmark of Simonidean style. The Greek term for this aesthetic is ἀκρίβεια,[15] a word of double reference: the Greek lexicon defines ἀκρίβεια as "minute care about details of language, exact expression" or "minute care about financial expense, miserliness." Practices of life and practices of language overlap on an epitaphic stone.

[13] Aristotle *Nicomachean Ethics* 1133b11–13.

[14] Bourdieu (1985), 55–61; Chantraine (1950), 112; Day (1989), 21, 24–28; Knox (1968); Nagy (1983), 46–48; Raubitschek (1968), 23–25; Svenbro (1988), 13–19; cf. also Letoublon (1995), 12.

[15] Dionysios of Halikarnassos *De imitatione* 2.420. The Aristophanic scholiast (on *Peace* 695ff.) uses a parallel term, σμικρολογία, whose referents similarly include "verbal precision" and "stinginess with money."

We have no certain information on how Simonides arrived at the price for a poem. Did he calculate number of verses? Number of words? Number of letters? Or perhaps allusions to Homer, metrical nicety, original figures of speech? Historians do not have answers to such questions; there are no literary contracts extant from the fifth century B.C. But Simonides composed a great many of his poems for inscription on stone and we do know something about the art of epigraphy in this period. In fact it was the period of highest development in ancient engraving techniques. As local Greek alphabets found their way to regularization, letter shapes became more precise and engravers began to develop a care for the aesthetics of inscription. They were thinking about details like the proportions of the stone, how to place the text on the stone at a height convenient for the reader to read, how to use lettering of a different size in the heading for increased legibility and liveliness.[16] Some engravers liked to enhance the effect of an inscription by painting the letters after they were cut, using red paint or sometimes alternating lines of red and black. Moreover, a new precisionist style of inscriptional writing had developed in the time of the Persian Wars—perhaps as a consequence of the high demand for gravestones during these years—a style called στοι-χῆδον (*stoichēdon*). In *stoichēdon* style, letters are aligned vertically as well as horizontally and placed at equal intervals along their respective alignments like ranks of men in military formation.[17] This style came to perfection during Simonides' lifetime due to the introduction of an important technical advance, the chequer.

The chequer was a grid of horizontal and vertical lines marked on the stone before cutting so as to divide its surface into equal rectangles. The text could then be engraved in perfect *stoichēdon* sequence by placing one letter in each rectangular space. Using the chequer, the engraver could fix precisely the point to which his text would run on the stone. Historians tells us that fifth-century engravers ruled out their stones beforehand with remarkable exactitude: they find that the margin of error on well-cut

[16] Woodhead (1959), 89–90.
[17] Austin (1938), 1.

stones due to variation in size of the chequer unit is not more than half a millimeter.[18]

Physical facts do influence artistic and cognitive design. Whether or not he was a miser, imagine how much time Simonides must have spent in his studio, drawing mental lines and positioning data, measuring off rectangles in his mind's eye, counting out letters and cutting away space, reckoning prices. Paul Celan once described the task of the poet as "measuring off the area of the given and the possible" (*den Bereich des Gegebenen und des Möglichen auszumessen*).[19] For Simonides, this measuring had a concrete professional and technical dimension. Surely there is a kinship between the physical facts of the stone and the stylistic facts of the language. Reasoning with stone will have trained ἀκρίβεια into all his practices of hand, eye and mind. Reasoning with the demands of the market will have channeled this precision along certain lines. Money offers a design for thought. To the extent that the language of his verse is filled with counting, numbers and quantification, with references to limit and loss, with metaphors of debit, credit and gratuity, you could say he conceives of human life in terms of economic relation. One of his best-known epitaphs summarizes the relation in a single sentence: "We are all debts owed to Death."[20]

This sentence is an important one for Simonides himself and for the whole epitaphic tradition. The idea that human life is not a gift but a loan or a debt, which will have to be paid back, originated with Simonides. It became a cliché on gravestones throughout Hellenistic and Roman times; numerous examples are extant.[21] But in Simonides' phrasing the idea has a bleakness that sets it apart. Facts of stone and money alone cannot account for this sentence. I think we must trace it back to a hard early decision.

Simonides was born on the island of Keos: a barren, rocky, impoverished place where the calculus of sheer survival demanded

---

[18] Ibid., 31.

[19] Reply to a questionnaire from the Flinker Bookstore, Paris, 1958: Celan (1990), 22; Waldrop (1986), 16.

[20] Simonides fr. 79 *FGE; Palatine Anthology* 10.105.2.

[21] Lattimore (1962), 15–18.

of its inhabitants an economy both radical and obvious. It was the custom on Keos for every male citizen who reached the age of sixty to voluntarily drink the hemlock, in order that there be enough supplies of life to go round. The historian Strabo records the rationale for this custom in a sentence as cold and clear as an epitaph:

The man who cannot live well shall not live poorly.[22]

Simonides chose to live elsewhere. Emigrating early from his homeland, the poet spent his life traveling about the Greek world to the houses of various aristocratic patrons and survived until well into his nineties on what we might call borrowed time. I cannot help but wonder how these actuarial matters affected his poetic style, as the years passed over him and Death failed to call in its debt. I suppose a poet writes on the world according as the world writes on a poet. You may know the story told of Paul Celan, that he returned after a weekend away from home one Monday morning of 1942 to find his house sealed and his parents removed.[23] They had been deported to a death camp in the Ukraine. He never saw them again. Arguably, this sudden excision remained the subject of his verse to the end of his life. In a postwar poem (called "Deathshroud")[24] addressed to his mother, he says,

Was du aus Leichtem wobst,
trag ich dem Stein zu Ehren.

[That which you wove out of light stuff
I wear in honor of stone.]

The stone that the poet honors here is his mother's grave marker, but also the plane surface of life from which she was carved away. The garment of light stuff that she wove into a shroud for herself has become the texture of his own memory.

For a poet like Simonides, who made his living by honoring stones in this way, excision is a physical process that becomes a

22 Strabo 10.486.
23 Chalfen (1991), 146–48, and see below, Chapter IV.
24 Celan (1983), 1:53; (1988), 68–69.

mode of meaning. It involves the carving of stone and voice and remembrance. Let us consider how:

ΣΑΜΑ	TOMB
ΤΟΔΕ	THIS
ΣΠΙΝΘΗΡ	SPINTHER
ΣΠΙΝΘΗΡ᾽	UPON SPINTHER
ΕΠΕΘΗΚΕ	SET
ΘΑΝΟΝΤΙ	DEAD

Simonides composed this single sentence for the gravestone of a certain Spinther.[25] Nothing is known about Spinther, neither his provenance, date, ancestry, nor what compunction moved him to commission his own epitaph. His nonentity is an important factor in assessing his epitaphic investment; Spinther would have vanished utterly save for a single Simonidean line of verse. But note that Simonides has not just saved Spinther's life, he has doubled it.

First, look at the stone. The verse was probably inscribed on the stone as a block of words vertically aligned in *stoichēdon* sequence. The inscription may have been painted in alternating lines of red and black. If so, an ancient Greek reader will notice an economical fact. The single verse contains two epitaphs. The red letters (TOMB SPINTHER SET) make one sentence and the black letters (THIS UPON SPINTHER DEAD) make another.

Now let us take the measure of letters a little deeper. Look at the syntax. On the epitaph the word Σπίνθηρ is a noun in the nominative case that stands as subject of the sentence directly on top of Σπίνθηρ᾽, a noun in the dative case that is indirect object of the sentence. Spinther's action as agent of the verb ἐπέθηκε ("set") is to confer a "tomb" (σῆμα) upon his own dead self. The

---

[25] Although the *Palatine Anthology* regards the poem as incomplete and leaves a space for a missing pentameter, Page believes it is an early single-hexameter epigram of the type illustrated by Friedländer and Hoffleit (1948), 9ff.: Simonides fr. 86 *FGE; Palatine Anthology* 7.177.

Page prints a slightly duller text (reading Σπίνθηρι πατὴρ for Σπίνθηρ Σπίνθηρ᾽), which he judges "primitive and artless." Edmonds (1927) suggests the text I have printed above: Simonides fr. 155; it may be wrong (Edmonds is a maverick editor), but it seems closer in spirit to the otherwise rarely artless Simonides.

Greek word σῆμα can also mean "sign": Spinther's epitaph signi-
fies that in some sense he is not after all a dead object, for the
syntax of his relationship to mortality is changed by the action of
the verse. Notice the difference between Σπίνθηρ and Σπίνθηρ'.
Metrics require Spinther's name in the dative case (properly
Σπίνθηρι) to be elided of its final vowel before conjunction with
the initial vowel of the following verb ἐπέθηκε. This produces
Σπίνθηρ', which sounds just like Σπίνθηρ: as if the poem could
reinflect Spinther from dative dependence on death to double
subjectivity in his own sentence—just for an instant *Spinther' Spin-
ther* imitates himself in a semantic friction that generates two lives
from one death and two men from one name. Loss and profit
change places in Simonides' economy of grace.[26]

Grace makes an epitaph brilliant to read, grace makes it memo-
rable. Imagine how it would happen, if you were a wandering
passerby who stopped to read Spinther's last words one day in the
fifth century B.C.

Ancient inscriptions were truly "talking stones," in the sense
that silent reading was not a usual nor a practical mode of de-
ciphering them.[27] Generally inscribed in *scriptio continua* with no
spaces between the words, stones demanded to be read aloud so
that the reader could "recognize" (ἀναγιγνώσκειν) the words.
What is recognized in such reading is not individual letters or
visual facts so much as a sequence of sounds ordered *in viva voce*
as the reader hears himself pronounce them. Words and word
groups obscure to the eye will shape themselves upon the ear and
unlock the codes of memory. So the verbs for "to read" in Greek
typically begin with a prefix like ἀνα- ("again") or ἐπι- ("on top
of") as if reading were essentially regarded as a sort of sympa-
thetic vibration between letters composed by a writer and the

---

[26] I have used an apostrophe to make Spinther's elision clear in my text;
however, it is not certain whether, or how, ancient stonecutters would have indi-
cated such a thing on a stone. It is possible the iota was carved on the stone and
elided only in voice, but this messes up an otherwise perfect *stoichēdon* pattern.
On the question of iota in general, and why stonecutters disliked cutting this
letter especially at the end of a line, see Austin (1938), 104, 111.

[27] Bourdieu (1985); Chantraine (1950); Knox (1968); Nagy (1983); Svenbro
(1988).

voice in which a reader pulls them out of silence.[28] It is interesting that the second most conspicuous feature of Simonides' style (after exactitude) in the opinion of ancient critics is a quality they call τὸ συμπαθές.[29] Generally translated into English as "sympathy" or "pathos," the term implies some shared movement of soul between writer and reader, as if words could have a power to enter the reader and design an emotion there from inside his own voice.[30]

It is your voice you hear performing an act of elision upon Spinther. It is you who realize, even as you vocalize the name a second time, that you have to excise the vowel relating Spinther-subject to Spinther-object, Spinther present to Spinther past. It is you who pronounce him "dead" (*thanonti*) and fall silent. Then turn and walk away.

People who knew Paul Celan say he never put aside the guilt of having survived his parents in 1942.[31] There are no data on how Simonides felt about "jumping the line" to get out of Keos before his hour of hemlock arrived. The responsibility of the living to the dead is not simple. It is we who let them go, for we do not

---

[28] It is fashionable to interpret this relationship between written text and reader's voice as a "question of power" (Bourdieu in Chartier [1985], 235; Svenbro [1988], 53), wherein the reader is dispossessed of his own voice in order to facilitate realization of the inscription, or even as a "point neuralgique" (Svenbro [1988], 207), whose structure replicates the paederastic model of dominance and submission that is presently seen to inform so many aspects of the ancient Greek cultural experiment. "La voix se soumettre à la trace écrite," says Svenbro, who characterizes the reader's "service" to the writer by direct analogy with the homosexual act of love and its dark emotions of use. "Lire, c'est prêter son corps à un scripteur peut-être inconnu, pour faire resonner des paroles 'étrangères,' 'd'autrui,' *allotrioi*" (213). The remarkable humorlessness of this line of interpretation seems to belie not only the terms in which the ancients themselves speak of written works of art (e.g., *poiema, kosmos, charis*), but also the spirit of freedom in which artists like Simonides play through the possibilities of meaning available conjointly to writer and reader within a piece of language. Perhaps exchange of power need not always mean abuse of power. Meaning, after all, exists to be exchanged.

[29] *Vita Aeschyli* 119.

[30] Cf. Quintilian's *miseratio commovenda* ("Pity moving together with pity"): *Institutio oratoria* 10.1.64.

[31] Felstiner (1995), 14–15; Washburn and Guillemin (1986), vii.

accompany them. It is we who hold them here—deny them their nothingness—by naming their names. Out of these two wrongs comes the writing of epitaphs.

MOTION

Epitaphs create a space of exchange between present and past by gaining a purchase on memory. Simonides, whose expertise in the mnemonic art was examined in the previous chapter, seems to have given considerable thought to the space of memory and to how words furnish it. He understands that to make a mental space memorable, you put into it movement, light and unexpectedness. In Spinther's case the movement is very bright indeed: his name is also the Greek word for "spark." Like a spark struck by rubbing two coins together, Spinther is sent flying forward to perpetuate his own significance beyond the grave. Let us look now at another example where Simonides shows us memory as an event pulled out of darkness by language: exchange of blue death for fireproof fame.

ἄσβεστον κλέος οἵδε φίληι περὶ πατρίδι θέντες
   κυάνεον θανάτου ἀμφεβάλοντο νέφος·
οὐδὲ τεθνᾶσι θανόντες, ἐπεί σφ᾽ ἀρετὴ καθύπερθε
   κυδαίνουσ᾽ ἀνάγει δώματος ἐξ Ἀίδεω.[32]

[Asbestos glory these men set around their dear fatherland
   and in a dark blue death cloud they wrapped themselves.
Not dead having died. Because virtue down from above
   keeps pulling them up glorying out of Hades' house.]

"Glory" here is an asbestos energy that works itself out through the surfaces of the words, like the glow from a funeral pyre. There are different surfaces, which open and shift as unexpectedly as smoke. There are questions and answers, mysteriously disoriented from one another. What is burning? Apparently not that which has been set on fire. Who is dead? Apparently not those who have died. Out of these mysteries the poet creates a general mood of

---

[32] Simonides fr. 9 *FGE; Palatine Anthology* 7.251

disorientation, which is spatial, aural and temporal as well as cognitive. The reader has the sense that he is staring down into a tomb. He is listening hard, he is expecting to hear a door slam shut. Instead he hears his own voice open and stall on the unusually[33] awkward hiatus of vowels between "death" (θανάτου) and "wrapped themselves" (ἀμφιβάλοντο) at the middle of the poem. As he looks *down from above* at the doorway of death, he is expecting to see darkness. Instead there is a passageway out of which very bright living beings are rising and keep rising *up* into the moment of his own reading. The verb tenses control this action, moving from the aorist instant of death described in the first couplet ("set," "wrapped"), to a verb in the perfect tense denying the closure of death at the center ("not dead having died"), to end in the present progressive ("keeps pulling") like a slow leak of immortality. A final gaping vowel (Ἀίδεο) at the very end of the poem leaves Hades' house standing open. Losing life upward.

Paul Celan wrote only one explicit epitaph, for the death of his infant son in 1953 ("Epitaph for François").[34] Like Simonides' poem, it is located in a space between two worlds. But for Celan this is a space to be crossed in only one direction. He makes us hear the doors slam shut:

GRABSCHRIFT FÜR FRANÇOIS

Die beiden Türen der Welt
stehen offen:
geöffnet von dir
in der Zwienacht.
Wir hören sie schlagen und schlagen
und tragen das ungewisse,
und tragen das Grün in dein Immer.

Oktober 1953

[EPITAPH FOR FRANÇOIS

The two doors of the world
stand open:

---

[33] See Page (1981), 200.
[34] Celan (1983), 1:105; (1988), 78–79.

opened by you
in the twinight.
We hear them slam and slam
and carry the thing that's uncertain
and carry the green thing into your Ever.

October 1953]

This is the only poem Celan ever published with its date under-
neath. Its premise is precision. The poet's neologism *Zwienacht*
("twinight"), made out of the number two and the noun for night,
counts out the moment of death. There is no question, these doors
close. We hear them slam and slam (*schlagen und schlagen*). The
sound echoes through the final verse (*und tragen . . . und tragen*)
into eternity. Like Simonides, Celan uses syntactical choices as well
as sound effects to draw the reader into the mood of the epitaphic
situation: we watch helplessly as the green adjective of life (*das
Grün*) disappears into an everlasting adverb (*dein Immer*) once and
for all. Like Simonides, Celan constructs his epitaph as an act of
attention shared between poet and reader, which moves out from
the reader's voice through all the surfaces of the poet's language.
But the mood is simpler and the direction is down.

Simonides prefers to treat time as a two-way corridor. He seems
confident in the power of "virtue" to pull open the door at this
end and reverse the natural direction of mortal traffic. Such con-
fidence is a typical feature of the epitaphic rhetoric of his nu-
merous public monuments. Also ascribed to his name are memo-
rials for dead men at the battles of Plataia, Thermopylai, Dirphys,
Artemision, Salamis, Marathon, Eurymedon, Tanagra, as well as
other monuments to classical violence, like the cenotaph honor-
ing Leonidas at Sparta and the statue commemorating Harmo-
dios and Aristogeiton at Athens. The language of these civic com-
missions makes clear what kind of ideological negotiation was
going on in the mid-fifth century between the city and its own acts
of blood. Public epitaphic rhetoric by and large avoids the regis-
ter of pity in order to emphasize an activity of praise.[35] We can call
this emphasis deliberate in virtue of its contrast with the epitaphic

---

[35] Loraux (1986), 47–56; but cf. Day (1989), who would deemphasize claims
to pity on the private epitaphs.

verse that Simonides wrote for private persons, which is suffused with pity. Tears do not figure in the public epitaphs. These poems are encomia, not laments. They posit an active choice, not a passive suffering, of death and express transcendent faith in the value of the choice: glory (*kleos*) is the measure of value. No door slams shut on it.

Rules change when Simonides turns his attention to the smaller, sadder ghostliness of a private tomb. The epitaph inscribed to Megakles gives a sense of constriction rather than openness, of grief kept secret. Tears, no glory:

σῆμα καταφθιμένοιο Μεγακλέος εὖτ᾽ ἂν ἴδωμαι,
   οἰκτίρω σε, τάλαν Καλλία, οἷ᾽ ἔπαθες.[36]

[Whenever I see the tomb of dead Megakles
   I pity you, sad Kallias, what you suffered.]

The emotion of the poem is eerily three-cornered and works by deflection. It moves out from the reader to touch Megakles' tomb but is then bounced off Megakles onto a third, unanticipated presence. Kallias materializes silently by the reader's side, more mysterious and more pitiable than the dead man. It is as if you were standing alone (you thought) in a room and suddenly heard someone breathing. The painting of Giotto called *Joachim Retiring to His Sheepfold* shows Joachim, after his expulsion from the temple in Jerusalem, arriving back at his sheepfold into the presence of two shepherds with their sheep and a small jumping dog. Joachim is in deep dejection and fixes his eyes on the ground, evidently unconscious of his surroundings. It is a moment of profound emotion, which Giotto has painted in such a way as to deliberately disorient the viewer's perception of it. For as we contemplate Joachim, our sympathy for him is intercepted by the shepherd, who is staring straight out of the painting "towards us, sympathetically, as though we had all witnessed a disaster together."[37] The shep-

---

[36] Simonides fr. 75 *FGE; Palatine Anthology* 7.511. But the poem is so strange that completeness, authenticity and genre remain in dispute. "Manifesto mutilatum" (Bergk); "of course not a fragment" (Wilamowitz); Page (1981), 295.

[37] Meiss (1960), 6; see also Barasch (1987), 42–44; Trost (1964), 26 and pl.

herd's stare has a strange tension—at once gathering us into the suffering of Joachim and setting up a barrier that keeps it private. The shepherd's eye makes contact with our sympathy but also marks the place where sympathy stops short. Joachim's grief is and remains beyond us. In somewhat the same way, Simonides' three-cornered epigram makes one spare fact explicit: the privacy of grief. No one else can really know what Kallias suffered when he lost Megakles.

MEASURE

All Simonides' epitaphic poems take the form of elegiac couplets. It will be worthwhile to reflect on why this is so. First let us consider how elegiacs work.

Elegiac meter is a distich form, that is, made of two verses of different types in regular alternation. Each verse is followed by a pause and the distich may be repeated any number of times. The elegiac distich consists of a hexameter (six-beat) verse followed by a type of pentameter (five-beat) verse that is made by duplication of the *hemiepes* or first half of a hexameter. Note that the two halves of the pentameter are interchangeable, both ending in a disyllable. In other words, every elegiac couplet has a unit of hexameter followed by this same unit broken into two equal halves balanced against one another—the acoustic shape of a perfect exchange. Nice to think of these exchanges also marked visually (as suggested above) by painting them in alternating lines of red and black. Rhythmically, the elegiac couplet resembles a pendulum: it moves out, moves back, by its own momentum, wasting nothing. Economy of breath in motion.

When verse began to be seen on Greek monuments in the seventh century B.C., various meters were used (with hexameter predominating) but a trend began at Athens under the Peisistratids to emphasize the elegiac couplet. From the early sixth century, elegiac became the canonical meter for inscribed verses of any literary or social pretension.[38] I would guess that Simonides, who

---

[38] Wallace (1984), 315.

flourished in Peisistratid Athens, was instrumental in this canon-
ization. Let me solidify this conjecture with two further examples
of his mastery of elegiac form. His ability to manipulate form in
the service of fact suggests to me a special affinity between the
poet and this very distinctive metrical idea, the elegiac.

We still do not know quite how to read the inscription he wrote
for the sensational statues of Harmodios and Aristogeiton in
Athens. Although it is not an epitaph, this monument commemo-
rates the deaths of three people: Harmodios, Aristogeiton and
Hipparchos.[39] It was erected probably soon after 510 B.C., on the
occasion of the expulsion of Hippias, brother of Hipparchos and
so-called last tyrant of Athens. Hippias was driven out of the city in
510 in a complicated coup engineered by the Alkmaionid family.
But political rivals of the Alkmaionids were soon scheming to de-
fraud them of credit for this action and a myth began to be gener-
ated ascribing the "liberation of Athens" to two young men
named Harmodios and Aristogeiton.

These two men had in fact murdered Hippias' brother, Hip-
parchos, three years before.[40] The real motive for this murder, as
historians since Thucydides attest, was homosexual jealousy.[41] Ac-
cording to Thucydides, Harmodios and Aristogeiton were lovers.
When Hipparchos, the brother of the tyrant, became enamored
of the young Harmodios and made overtures to him, Harmodios
reported the matter to his lover, who took immediate action. Aris-
togeiton organized a conspiracy to assassinate Hipparchos along
with his powerful brother amid the crowds and confusion on the
city streets of Athens during the annual Panathenaic procession.
The conspirators did in fact succeed in dispatching Hipparchos
according to plan, but then the bodyguards of Hippias appeared

[39] An overview of the archaeological evidence for the statues of Harmodios
and Aristogeiton as well as further bibliography may be found in Thompson and
Wycherly (1972). For more detailed studies, see Brunnsåker (1955); Taylor
(1981). Ancient testimonia for the statue group is collected in Thompson
(1957), 93–98.

[40] See [Plato] *Hipparchus* 228a; the Parian Marble A 45; Attic skolia 893–96
PMG.

[41] Thucydides 6.54–60; Page (1981), 186–88.

and cut Harmodios down. Aristogeiton was captured alive, imprisoned, tortured and later executed.

Neither the events of this romantic tragedy nor its confused aftermath can be shown to have provoked the political action that ousted Hippias three years later. Yet soon after the expulsion,[42] a statue of Harmodios and Aristogeiton as "liberators of Athens" was set up in the Athenian agora, inscribed with a couplet allegedly by Simonides:

ἦ μέγ' Ἀθηναίοισι φόως γένεθ' ἡνίκ' Ἀριστο-
γείτων Ἵππαρχον κτεῖνε καὶ Ἁρμόδιος.[43]

[Surely a great light for the Athenians came into being when
   Aristogeiton and Harmodios killed Hipparchos.]

Translation cannot convey the verbal tensions of the Greek original. The first verse sets up "a great light" surrounding "the Athenians" on both sides. The second verse shows us Hipparchos stranded between Aristogeiton and Harmodios as the direct object of their verb "killed"; the verb is singular, despite its compound subject, to emphasize this unit of murderous enclosure. Simonides renders the impassioned facts of the story as structure rather than surface rhetoric. We may presume that his commission was to glorify the murder as disinterested democratic action. Yet he has managed to suggest the darker pressure of a private erotic agenda behind political myth.

It is a story of close cuts and deadly contiguities. It is an epigram that begins with "a remarkable breach of one of the most fundamental rules of elegiac verse."[44] The rule that a word boundary

[42] If Page is correct that the monument was erected during the period when the Alkmaionid Kleisthenes had been driven out of Athens by his rival Isagoras (508/7): see Page (1981), 187.

[43] Simonides fr. 1 *FGE*. The monument was removed from Athens to Persia in 480, then replaced with a new monument and reinscribed in 477/6: Pausanias 1.8.5; Pliny *Natural History* 34.70. It is not known whether the present epigram, ascribed to Simonides by Hephaistion, was composed for the first or the second monument.

[44] Page (1981), 188. See also Van Raalte (1986), 64; Kassel (1975), 211–18.

should invariably occur at verse end is first stated by Hephaistion, the lexicographer to whom we owe preservation of this poem. "Every metrical line ends in a complete word, hence such verses as these from the epigrams of Simonides are incorrect," says Hephaistion.[45] This incorrect prosodic impulse permits Aristogeiton to overstep his place in the hexameter verse and join his beloved in the next line as they close in upon the intrusive Hipparchos. But every license has a price. The structure of the elegiac couplet divides Aristogeiton's name in half as violently as jealousy did cut through his life.

The physical facts of the monument on which this epigram was inscribed may have emphasized some of these tensions, by an interplay between text and figures. Neither the statue itself nor any detailed ancient description is extant but a number of copies have been identified. It seems clear that the two figures stood side by side, forming a vigorous composition with Simonides' epigram inscribed below.[46] We are in fact able to visualize how the epigram looked due to the discovery, in the Athenian agora in 1936, of a base of Pentelic marble containing the end of the pentameter verse of this couplet.[47] Simonides' text will then have run continuously across the base from left to right beneath the two statues. The first half of Aristogeiton's name would be cut directly under his own figure, surging forward on the left with sword raised in the direction of Harmodios. And the latter half of the name thrusts itself across the gap between the two figures, with the gestural energy appropriate to a lover ousting a rival from his beloved's side. Now it is true (and no Greek reader of the epigram would be unaware) that the name Aristogeiton, with its opening iambic rhythm, scans awkwardly no matter where you put it in a dactylic hexameter. But I would suggest that the way Simonides plays this acoustic fact into his design is meant to tell us less about metrical recalcitrance than about emotions of murder in a paede-

[45] Hephaistion *Encheiridion* 28.

[46] Richter (1929), 200–201.

[47] Meritt (1936), 355–56 believes this stone to be from the base of the second monument (477 B.C.) with an inscription copied from the original (510 B.C.) base.

rastic police state. His exactitude has a sculptural power to carry the reader's eye around the back of the forms into human causes. Here again we see the "sympathy" for which Simonides was celebrated arising directly from the physical facts of his ἀκρίβεια.

And surely this is one function of great poetry, to remind us that human meaning does not stop with the physical facts. Facts live in their relation to one another; and language is able to objectify facts insofar as it can name (or as the Greeks say, imitate) these relations. When we speak of the Simonidean quality of sympathy as a function of this poet's exactitude, we are at the root of his notion that "the word is a picture of things." We are recognizing his ability to make the same relations occur among a set of words in a poem as obtain among a set of facts in the world. "To chew this bread with writing teeth," as Paul Celan calls it.[48] Let us consider another example of such imitative action in an epitaph composed by Simonides for a woman named Archedike:

ἀνδρὸς ἀριστεύσαντος ἐν Ἑλλάδι τῶν ἐφ' ἑαυτοῦ
   Ἱππίου Ἀρχεδίκην ἥδε κέκευθε κόνις,
ἣ πατρός τε καὶ ἀνδρὸς ἀδελφῶν τ' οὖσα τυράννων
   παίδων τ' οὐκ ἤρθη νοῦν ἐς ἀτασθαλίην.[49]

[Of a man who himself was best in Greece of the men of his day:
   Hippias' daughter Archedike this dust hides,
She of a father, of a husband, of brothers, of children all tyrants
   being.
Nor did she push her mind up into presumption.]

Archedike was the daughter of Hippias (last tyrant of Athens, as above), a man whose presence and power, accompanied by all the rest of the men of his day in the first verse of the poem, effectively buries Archedike in the middle of the second verse, boxed in between her father's name and the dust of her own grave. The third verse locates her total claim to fame in a participle—"being"—and specifies the mode of her being in virtue of its fourfold relation to men. It is noteworthy that this claim, which informs us

[48] In the poem "Mit den Sackgassen": Celan (1983), 2:358.
[49] Simonides fr. 26 FGE; Thucydides 6.59.3.

Archedike played the roles of daughter, wife, sister and mother, does not use any of these nouns to designate her. Archedike's functions are indicated exclusively by her grammatical dependence on the nouns father, husband, brother, children. The fourth verse does at last ascribe a quality to Archedike but it is a quality named for its absence. This woman's lack of presumption comes as little surprise at the end of an epitaph that refers every aspect of her being to male derivation. True to its word, the poem hides all but Archedike's "dust."

There are a number of (by now familiar) things one could say at this point about masculine discourse and patriarchal codes and the suppression of female voice. Simonides, I suspect, had none of them in mind when he composed this poem but was in fact entertaining quite other, honorific purposes with a measurable success. And therefore the epitaph to Archedike may stand as an all the more heartening evidence that a poet who forms his attention in exactitude can end up telling more truth than he means to. For he is drawn ever more deeply to the inside of the physical facts. As Rilke says, "Like a drink through thirst, gravity plunges through him."[50] The act of poetic attention gathers to itself a directional force as mysterious as gravity from the poet's instinct for true relationships.

The Greeks of the generation into which Simonides was born had a name for this instinct and a profound faith in its truth-claim. They called the instinct that makes a poet a poet simply σοφία ("wisdom"). They believed the exercise of poetic wisdom to be the clearest place where truth can obtain existence for itself. You and I, on the other hand, belong to a generation that is no longer able to use such a word nor command such a belief. To cite a phrase used by Paul Celan in his Bremen speech, we are people "wounded by and seeking reality" (*wirklichkeitswund und Wirklichkeit suchend*).[51] He does not speak of poetic wisdom and seems uncertain of his readers' tolerance for truth. "We live un-

[50] "Schwerkraft," in Rilke (1963), 2:179.
[51] Celan (1990), 39; Waldrop (1986), 35.

der dark skies and there are few human beings. Hence . . . few poems. The hopes I have left are small."[52] Nonetheless, with his small hopes, Celan addressed himself to issues of sympathy, exactitude and memory, as Simonides did. He wrote no further epitaphs (after François') but he does seem at times to have entertained the notion that the dead can save the living.

CELAN

An epitaph is a way of thinking about death and gives consolation. Our minds seek shelter from a world of barely controlled flux in such forms of order. The ancient epitaphic order, brought to perfection by Simonides, sets up a mimesis of exchange whose consolations are not only rhythmic and conceptual but something more. Salvation occurs, through the act of attention that forms stone into memory, leaving a residue of greater life. I am speaking subjectively. There is no evidence of salvation except a gold trace in the mind. But this trace convinces me that the beautiful economic motions of Simonides' epitaphic verse capture something essential to human language, to the give and take of being, to what saves us.

In the Meridian speech, Celan talks about the motions of poetic language as if they were pendular: "The poem holds its own on its own margin. In order to endure it constantly calls out and pulls itself back from an 'already no more' into a 'still here.' "[53] These motions of exchange, which allow the poem to endure, are set out on facing pages of Celan's 1967 collection *Atemwende* as two opposing phases of the alchemical process. The poems "Solve" and "Coagula" treat several different topics, including the uses of language and the murder of Rosa Luxemburg, under the figure of alchemy:[54]

[52] Celan (1990), 32; Waldrop (1986), 26.

[53] *Das Gedicht behauptet sich am Rande seiner selbst; es ruft und holt sich, um bestehen zu können, unausgesetzt aus seinem Schon-nicht-mehr in sein Immer-noch zurück:* Celan (1990), 54; (1986), 48.

[54] Celan (1983), 2:82 and 83.

Solve

Entosteter, zu
Brandscheiten zer-
spaltener Grabbaum:

an den Gift-
pfalzen vorbei, an den Domen,
stromaufwärts, strom-
abwärts geflößt

vom winzig-lodernden, vom
freien
Satzzeichen der
zu den unzähligen zu
nennenden un-
aussprechlichen
Namen aus-
einandergeflohenen, ge-
borgenen
Schrift.

Coagula

Auch deine
Wunde, Rosa.

Und das Hörnerlicht deiner
rumänischen Büffel
an Sternes Statt überm
Sandbett, im
redenden, rot-
aschengewaltigen
Kolben.

[Solve

DisEastered
gravetree split
up for logburning:

96

past the poison-
palatinates, past the cathedrals,
streamupwards, stream-
downwards rafted

by tiny-blazing, by
free
punctuation marks of the
saved writing
that has flowed asunder
into the uncountable
unsayable
to be said
names.]

[COAGULA

Also your
wound, Rosa.

And the hornlight of your
Romanian buffaloes
instead of stars above the
sandbed, in the
talking red-
ash powerful
butt.]

Solve and *coagula* are Latin imperative verbs that refer to two
stages of the alchemical process: "Separate!" and "Recombine!" In
alchemical recipes these verbs are usually in the plural. *Solvite cor-*
pora et coagulate spiritum, says Nicholas Valois.[55] Celan has singu-
larized the command perhaps because, to judge from the first
verse of the second poem, he is addressing Rosa herself—one
philosopher of the saving of matter to another. Within alchemical
practice, "solution" is an initial separation of the elements of the

[55] Olsson (1994), 269; on alchemical terms and practice, see also Jung
(1953), 228–32; Taylor (1930), 109–40.

prima materia. This stage, in which the elements turn black and undergo a "death," was called *nigredo* by alchemists. "Coagulation" is a final stage of solidification and the goal of the process. It occurs after "resurrection" of the elements and is signaled by the color red, thus called *rubedo.* Calling out and pulling back, the movement of the poems is from black to red, from logs to ash, from written marks to Rosa's wound. Elements of prime matter that suffer solution in the first poem include Christianity, for the tree of Easter is cut up into logs and floats away; and naming, for the punctuation marks that separate writing into nameable names are on fire: it all flows asunder.

In the second poem all this dissolution stops and goes solid. Christ's disavowed Easter pain congeals in Rosa's wound. Moving fires steady down as ash. Dispersed script takes the deadly form of a talking rifle butt. These features of "Coagula" may be analyzed in their double reference to the alchemical code and to the history of Rosa Luxemburg.[56] A mysticism of roses and suffering is found in the earliest Greek alchemical texts, but also evokes the head wound dealt to Rosa Luxemburg in her last hour. "Stars above the sandbed" may allude to a sign in the sky traditionally sought by alchemists at the end of the *nigredo* phase. Celan replaces this sign with "hornlight of your Romanian buffaloes." One critic finds here a reference to a letter of Rosa Luxemburg with which Celan was familiar. In the letter she describes a sight glimpsed from the window of her prison cell: wild water buffaloes, captured in Romania to be used instead of oxen as draught animals, were pulling an army cart into the prison yard and got stuck in the gate. A soldier in charge was using the heavy end of his whip to beat the animals until "the blood ran from their wounds." With deepest pity she remarks on how hard it is to lacerate buffalo hide, "proverbial for its toughness."[57]

Blood shows, in Rosa's last hour. Her captors struck her on the head with the end of a rifle and threw her in the Landwehr Canal.

[56] Olsson suggests also a reference to Rosa Leibovici, a friend of Celan's at Czernowitz: (1994), 274; Chalfen points out that Leibovici "came from Moldavia, home of the Romanian buffalo mentioned in the poem": (1979), 151.

[57] Olsson (1994), 270–71.

The final verses of the poem bring us to *rubedo,* to a terrible trans-mutation that does not have much in common with the noble process of alchemists who "healed" base metals into gold. Alchem-ical changes seem always to have been positive, never involving degradation except as an intermediate stage in a happier process. Celan is a man whose "hopes are small."[58] His poems do not pre-tend to partake of happier process or positive change. Yet he does set up an act of attention—pulled out of oblivion—that moves there and back and leaves some residue of greater life. So might the measures of Spinther's epitaph once have been set pulsing at the world in alternative verses of red and black. "Solve" and "Co-agula" do not constitute an epitaph, yet they do measure out a motion of exchange, pulling and calling. Neither Rosa Lux-emburg nor the uncountable names are saved by this motion. Except as writing. But that is not nothing.

[58] Above, note 49.

CHAPTER IV

Negation

SIMONIDES

"Nothing" is a good place to begin thinking about the economics of negation. It needs close thought. "But for want of that for which I am richer" is how Shakespeare's Cordelia puts it, after an argument with her father in which the two of them trade "nothing" back and forth five times like a bad coin.[1] "Nothing will come of nothing," Lear advises her[2]—but in fact a great deal comes of it before the end, and then nothing comes too. The word lends itself to scary word play, to unanswerable puns, to the sort of reasoning that turns inside out when you stare at it. Simonides and Paul Celan are both poets who enjoy this sort of reasoning and who orient themselves toward reality, more often than not, negatively.

In the case of Simonides, a negative orientation can be statistically shown. He says "No" more often than any other poet of his period. If we compare the extant corpus of his poetry, which contains roughly 1,300 legible words, with comparable samples of verse from the contemporary poets Anakreon, Pindar and Bakkhylides, the following statistic emerges: in 1,300 words of Anakreon we find the negative adverbs οὐ and μή employed 28 times; 1,300 words of Pindar render 16 usages of οὐ and μή; 1,300 words of Bakkhylides give us 19 instances of οὐ and μή. The count for Simonides is 56.

The high ratio of Simonidean negativity depends, in no small degree, on his inclination to form even positive statements negatively, that is, his fondness for the double negative. So, for example, when Simonides wishes to assert that human life contains

[1] Shakespeare, *King Lear* 1.1.229.
[2] Ibid. 1.1.89; cf. 1.4.125.

suffering, he says, "Nothing is not painful among men" (527 *PMG*) or "Not even the men of old who were sons of gods had lives that were not filled with pain and death and danger" (523 *PMG*). Instead of saying "Pleasure is good," he says, "Without pleasure not even a god's life is enviable" (584 *PMG*). Rather than "Virtue is difficult," he says, "No one attains virtue into whom heartbiting sweat does not come" (579 *PMG*). To describe a weeping woman he has the phrase, "with cheeks not unwet by tears" (543 *PMG*). To describe a sound that spreads far and wide, he says, "No leaf-shaking blast of wind arose that would have prevented the sound from spreading far and wide" (595 *PMG*). In order to celebrate the fact that the city of Tegea has survived a war, Simonides says, "The smoke of Tegea burning did not rise up into the clear air" (53 *FGE*). And in the famous poem known from Plato's *Protagoras*, Simonides addresses himself to the definition of virtue by setting out twelve negative and double-negative formulations in the space of forty lines of verse, leading to the resoundingly Spinozan conclusion, "All things to be sure are beautiful into which ugly things are not mixed" (542 *PMG*).[3]

It would be an insult to the care that this poet lavishes upon telling us what is not the case to dismiss his negativity as accidental, incidental or rhetorical. His poetic action insistently, spaciously and self-consciously[4] posits in order to deny. To read him is a repeated experience of loss, absence or deprivation for the reader who watches one statement or substantive after another snatched away by a negative adverb, pronoun or subordinate clause. Simonides' poetic imagination conjures so vividly events that did not occur, people who are not present, possibilities that cannot be expected, that these come to rival the reality that is present and actual. No other poet of the period manages to deny so much, so well. What is Simonides up to?

A prior question cannot be avoided. What is a negative?

---

[3] Hamilton (1899); cf. W. C. Fields: "Anyone who doesn't like children, dogs and horses can't be all bad."

[4] Self-awareness tautens, for example, fr. 593 *PMG:* "Not from fragrant painted flowers . . . but from the bitter thyme I suck my verse."

No Not Nothing

A negative is a verbal event. There are, philosophers assure us, no negatives in nature, where every situation is positively what it is. The negative is a peculiarly linguistic resource whose power resides with the user of words. But verbalization in itself is not sufficient to generate the negative. Negation depends upon an act of the imagining mind. In order to say "The smoke of Tegea burning did not rise up into the clear air," I bring together in my mind two pieces of data, one of which is present and actual (Tegea itself perceptible before me), the other of which is absent and fictitious (Tegea as it would be if it were burning). I put these two data together and say, "This is not that." Negation requires this collusion of the present and the absent on the screen of the imagination. The one is measured against the other and found to be discrepant; the discrepant datum is annihilated by a word meaning "No." The interesting thing about a negative, then, is that it posits a fuller picture of reality than does a positive statement.[5] So a person who speaks negatively can be said to command and display a more complete view of things than one who makes positive assertions. And a person who purchases a poem from a poet who uses three times as many negatives as anyone else can be said to be getting good value for his money.

Now the ancient poet is by definition someone who commands a fuller view of reality than other people. According to a venerable Greek tradition, the poet is σοφός ("wise") and his task is to see and to teach a vision of life from which the particularity of our ordinary experience ordinarily excludes us. But Simonides lived on the brink of a time when new and severe pressures would be placed on poetry to justify its claim to special wisdom. Simonides was a forerunner of what is called the Greek "enlightenment," that intense period of fifth-century intellectualism when the sophists launched their cri-

[5] "There is more and not less in the idea of an object conceived as 'not existing' than in the idea of this same object conceived as 'existing'; for the idea of the object as 'not existing' is necessarily the idea of the object as 'existing' with, in addition, the representation of an exclusion of this very object by the actual reality taken *en bloc*": Bergson (1928), 302.

tique of poetic wisdom and set about devising a science of dialectic to replace poetic teaching. Simonides seems to have anticipated the sophistic critique and coopted its science.

It was essentially a science of measurement, famously summarized by Protagoras in the words, "Man is the measure of all things—both of the things that are, that they are, and of the things that are not, that they are not."[6] Other fifth-century intellectuals would interest themselves in measuring geometrical angles, intervals of music, spaces between stars. Simonides predicted them all by locating his measuring inside the mind and method of poetic σοφία. And whereas Protagoras prided himself on a technical ability to argue both sides of any case and published two textbooks of *Contrary Arguments* (Ἀντιλογικά), Simonides constructed poems in the shape of *antilogika,* painting a picture of things that moves inclusively over the negative and the positive, defining the things that are by excluding the things that are not, evoking the absent in order to measure it against the present. The technique would impress any sophist but the poet's aim is not technical, nor is his meauring sophistic. It is a mode of knowledge,[7] perhaps best described in terms borrowed from philosophy. It was the fifth-century philosopher Parmenides who said to the seeker after truth, "You must gaze steadily at what is absent as if it were present by means of your mind."[8] It was the twentieth-

---

[6] Protagoras fr. B1 *VS;* and above, Chapter II. Cf. Plato *Theatetus* 161c; Aristotle *Metaphysics* 1062b13–18.

[7] Leopardi's poem "The Infinite" adopts a similar technique:

This lonely hill has always been so dear
to me and dear this hedge which hides away
the reaches of the sky. But sitting here
and wondering, I fashion in my mind
the endless spaces far beyond, the more
than human silences and deepest peace;
so that the heart is on the edge of fear.

One critic has said of these verses, "The very fact that the hedge cuts off the vision of unknowable space releases the imagination to create that vision": Casale (1981), 44.

[8] Parmenides fr. 4 *VS;* Bergson (1928), 289.

century philosopher Bergson who characterized philosophic speculation as "making use of the void to think the full." When Simonides pictures the world in relations of denial and absence, he is exercising traditional poetic σοφιά in a way that sets him apart. To a thinker like Protagoras, man is the criterion of what exists; his λόγος makes nothing of reality. The Simonidean λόγος says "No" to that nothing.[9]

Perhaps the plainest example of Simonides making use of the void in order to think the full is his tiny poem on time:

ἄνθρωπος ἐὼν μή ποτε φάσηις ὅ τι γίνεται αὔριον,
μηδ᾽ ἄνδρα ἰδὼν ὄλβιον ὅσσον χρόνον ἔσσεται·
ὠκεῖα γὰρ οὐδὲ τανυπτερύγου μυίας
οὕτως ἁ μετάστασις.[10]

[Being Man, you can't ever say what will happen tomorrow
nor, seeing a man prosper, how long it will last.
For swift—not even of a longwinged fly
so! the change.]

It is a poem so tiny it manages to vanish as you read it, not only into the past but into nonexistence. At the end you find yourself staring at an event that did not take place. The first three verses prepare this vanishing point by means of a series of contractions. As you proceed from verse 1 through verse 4, each line is shorter than the one before it. The units of syntax progressively simplify. The metrical units are reduced, from choriambic metra with dactylic expansion in verse 1, to choriambic metra alone in verse 2, to dactyls in verse 3 and finally, in verse 4, to an indefinable metrical shape not quite a choriamb not quite a dactyl. The units of thought dramatically diminish, from the universal ἄνθρωπος ("Man") of verse 1, to an individual ἄνδρα ὄλβιον ("prosperous man") in verse 2, who dwindles to a fly in verse 3, which vanishes in verse 4. And time itself shrinks sharply, from the foreverness of μή ποτε . . . αὔριον ("never . . . tomorrow") in verse 1, to a spe-

---

[9] Conversely (from a sophist of a more recent Enlightenment): "'Yes' said Mr. Casaubon, with that peculiar pitch of voice which makes the word half a negative" (George Eliot, *Middlemarch* [1965], 231).

[10] Fr. 521 *PMG*.

cific measurement of ὅσσον χρόνον ("how long") in verse 2, which contracts to a mere attribute of swiftness (ὠκεῖα) in verse 3, and even that vanishes in verse 4 into μετάστασις ("change"). *Metastasis* is where you end up but, by the time you get there, the change to which the word refers is not only retrospective, it is retrospectively negated. As you glance back from μετάστασις to the negative adverb οὐδὲ ("not even") looming above it, you realize that the fly in this poem has not only shifted its wings, it has flown right out of the argument, relegated to the category of a negative exemplum. Like time itself, the fly is present only as an absence.

The poet's control of time is a power vested in negativity. Once we have invented time, and we have, we can only escape it by refusing to know what time it is. An early painting of Cezanne's called *The Black Clock* is a painting of a clock with a face but no hands, a picture of timelessness. A clock without hands designates no particular time and all possible times at the same time. A clock without hands is a powerful image of the vantage-point taken by the poet as his λόγος ranges forward and backward in time and the rest of us stand, lodged in our partial view of reality, eyes fixed on the moment we call "the present." Meanwhile we should not overlook the fact that the clock face on which Cezanne captures timelessness is a black one: an act of painterly negation.[11]

To refuse to know what time it is, is an almost godlike gesture.[12] The mind that can deny time can say "No" to mortality, as Simonides did repeatedly and famously throughout his career, for he was the most prolific composer of epitaphs in the Greek tradition and widely celebrated for his funeral songs. It is a nice puzzle

[11] We might also recall the opening shot of Ozu's 1933 masterpiece Floating Weeds. This film concerns the effects of passing time on a traveling company of Kabuki players and begins in the waiting room of a railway station: the camera is positioned so that it looks out from inside the glass cabinet of an enormous stopped grandfather clock.

[12] Cf. Thomas Carlyle: "I was strong, of unknown strength, a spirit, almost a god. . . . Thus had the Everlasting No pealed authoritatively through all the recesses of my being, of my Me: and then it was that my whole Me stood up, in native God-created majesty and with emphasis recorded its Protest. Such a Protest, the most important transaction in life might be called" (*Sartor Resartus,* 8).

whether the outstanding negativity of this poet is cause or effect of the fact that he spent so much of his time in the company of The Great Gainsayer. Certainly death gives most of us our elemental experience of absent presence, and an epitaph might be thought of as a vanishing point—or a sort of concrete double negative—where the absence of life disappears into the presence of death and nullifies itself. Certainly the poet's power to negate the negating action of death derives from his special view of reality, a view that sees death everywhere and finds life within it, a view that perceives presence as absence and finds a way to turn the relation inside out. Certainly this paradox of absent presence, forming itself as an act of negation, is the shape built into Simonides' concepts and syntax and poetic technique, and into many of the stories he tells in his verse. Oddly, it also shapes the stories told *about* Simonides.

PRIVATE CUTS PUBLIC CUTS

What makes a poet, accident or attention? Maybe both. Let me recollect a few of the ancient anecdotes that place Simonides in situations of deprivation, refusal or loss. We have already seen Simonides seated at Hieron's board, waiting patiently as roast hare passes down the table to all the guests except himself; we have watched him watch the wine stewards mix snow into everyone else's wine except his own; we have heard tell that he kept two boxes in his house to store χάρις, physical and metaphysical grace, and that one box was always empty. We have remarked on the stinginess of his patron Skopas, who retracted half of Simonides' promised poetic fee; we have noted its miraculous aftermath, the erasure of Skopas and all his hall beneath a collapsed roof. These stories can be read as paradigms of what Marx called the richly contradictory nature of commodity exchange. For certainly money was the main accident of Simonides' life. And his attention to it sharpens the anecdotal contours of a very convincing poetic alienation. If we regard Simonides as someone smart enough to look both ways on the road that led from gifts to money, it is not surprising that he thought to align the contours of his own poetic persona with a sensational controversy of value that can never quite be dispelled from poetic production. To make up new stories is a waste of words, thought Celan's father. How would this father have regarded Simonides, who not only spent his life making up stories but is alleged to have added a third note to the lyre and invented four new letters for the Greek alphabet?

Did Simonides waste words? Yes! in the opinion of Skopas, who halved the poet's fee on the grounds that half his poem was irrelevant. This story, as recounted by Cicero and others, offers a remarkably plain allegory of the poet's relation to the problem of value. It is an axiom of economic theory since Marx that only by trying to sell his product in the market can a producer discover its objective value.[13] Marx describes a handloom weaver who works ten hours but (like Simonides) finds his work viewed in the marketplace as worth only half that. Ten hours of life become five hours of pay. What is striking in Marx's analysis of the issue is this insight: that to value a piece of work is to price the mortal span. When commodities present themselves to us for evaluation and exchange, Marx insists, what we are really measuring in them is time.[14]

Now in the Simonidean anecdote, the time factor is present from the beginning in the persons of the Dioskouroi—those divinities who halve immortality between them to avoid a mortal price—and is triumphant at the end in the feat of memory with which Simonides saves Skopas and his guests from obliteration. I have long puzzled over a sentence in the Simonidean testimonia that tells us:

παραινεῖ Σιμωνίδης παίζειν ἐν τῶι βίωι καὶ περὶ μηδὲν ἁπλῶς σπουδάζειν.[15]

[Simonides advises us to play at life and to be 100% serious about nothing.]

[13] Pilling (1980), 52–53.
[14] Marx (1867), 1:94.
[15] Fr. 646 *PMG*.

Now I begin to see what this sentence might mean. To be 100% serious about nothing, about absence, about the void which is fullness, is the destiny and task of the poet. The poet is someone who feasts at the same table as other people. But at a certain point he feels a lack. He is provoked by a perception of absence within what others regard as a full and satisfactory present. His response to this discrepancy is an act of poetic creation; he proceeds by means of his poetic σοφία to make present in the mind what is lacking from the actual. You might see it as a transcendent example of what Marx calls "surplus value," when a poet decides to double the negative of death and say "No" to oblivion. Or you might call it a waste of words.

CELAN

Celan, like Simonides, is a poet who comes to us wrapped in anecdotes that allegorize his relation to the word. One Friday evening in June 1942, so the story goes,[16] when weekend deportation action had begun against the Jewish population of Czernowitz, Paul Celan tried to convince his parents to hide out with him at a factory on the edge of town. They refused. He left without them. Returning Monday morning he found the house sealed and his parents removed. He never saw them again. To confront an empty space, where there were people the last time you looked, may make you think very concretely about negation. Celan, like Simonides standing on the threshold of an obliterated banquet hall, seems to have accepted the shock of sudden erasure as an assignment: to undertake lifelong thought about the operations of Yes and No.

A poem in which Celan expresses his commitment to this thought is "Sprich Auch Du,"[17] which begins:

Sprich auch du,
sprich als letzter,
sag deinen Spruch.

[16] Chalfen (1991), 146–47.
[17] Celan (1983), 1:135; (1988), 98–99.

Sprich—
Doch scheide das Nein nicht vom Ja.
Gib deinem Spruch auch den Sinn:
gib ihm den Schatten.

Gib ihm Schatten genug,
gib ihm so viel,
also du um dich verteilt weißt zwischen
Mittnacht und Mittag und Mittnacht.

[Speak so you,
speak as the last,
say your say.

Speak—
But split the No not from Yes.
Give your say also the sense:
give it the shadow.

Give it shadow enough,
give it as much
as you know is assigned to you between
midnight and midday and midnight.]

Perhaps addressing himself, Celan recommends a way of speaking that includes fullness and void, No and Yes, clockface and shadow. Time organizes his assignment of shadow: what you are really measuring here is that unit of change (or μετάστασις) which Simonides compares to the shift of a long-winged fly. Change means loss but a poet can defy it, holding both sides of the moment together, Friday night and Monday morning, absence and presence unsplit. The sentence in which Celan does so is carefully constructed:

Doch scheide das Nein nicht vom Ja.

"Keep yes and no unsplit," is how Michael Hamburger translates this. Yet the German word order does split *das Nein* from *Ja* by the negative adverb *nicht*. In between No and Yes Celan places the poet's power to cancel their difference, his license to double the negative of death. The poem's next stanza celebrates it:

109

Blicke umher:
sieh, wie's lebendig wird rings—
Beim Tode! Lebendig!
Wahr spricht, wer Schatten spricht.

[Look around:
see how it comes alive all round—
in death! Alive!
Speaks true who speaks shadow.]

Charged with the task of restoring a void, Simonides invented a mnemonic system whose order is spatial: you simply select a place and put the data in it as faces around a dining table. You defy the motions of time by holding life still in an instant of mind. Life shrinks, in Simonides' memory, to one perfectly economical room. In the final stanza of "Sprich Auch Du," Celan also talks of a shrinking of the world, and sees himself struggling to climb up to a vantage-point high above it, from which he can remember and speak. Instead of a memory-room, he describes a dark swimming space into which the poet places his data as precisely as if he were lowering a star on a thread.

Nun aber schrumpft der Ort, wo du stehst:
Wohin jetzt, Schattenentblößter, wohin?
Steige. Taste empor.
Dünner wirst du, unkenntlicher, feiner!
Feiner: ein Faden,
an dem er herabwill, der Stern:
um unten zu schwimmen, unten,
wo er sich schimmern sieht: in der Dünung
wandernder Worte.

[But now shrinks the place where you stand:
Where to now, shadestripped, where to?
Climb. Grope upwards.
Thinner you grow, more unknowable, finer!
Finer: a thread
on which it wants to descend, the star:
to swim down below, below
where it sees itself shimmer: in the swell
of wandering words.]

110

Celan closes with a distinction between abundance and economy, between the precision of his own word lowered on a finer and finer thread and the surge of wandering words that fills the world. His word has no excess, it is "shadestripped." And the mechanism of its economy is plain: Yes and No unsplit.

Before we explore the rationale of this mechanism more closely in Celan, let us consider an ancient example of it, from an epigram in which Simonides pictures the conditions that make a man something or nothing:

ἄνθωρωπ᾽, οὐ Κροίσου λεύσσεις τάφον· ἀλλὰ γὰρ ἀνδρός
χερνήτεω μικρὸς τύμβος, ἐμοὶ δ᾽ ἱκανός.[18]

[You! No you're not looking at Kroisos' tomb. Yes it's a poor
man's little mound, for me enough.]

The poem sets up an imaginary dialectic of wealth and poverty, of fame and nullity, of No and Yes. Kroisos was the last king of the fabulously wealthy kingdom of Lydia. When his armies were defeated by those of Kyros the Great, Kroisos piled his wealth up into a vast funeral pyre, placed himself on top and set it alight. No ancient Greek reader could hear this reference without seeing flames in his mind's eye. But Simonides' poem trains our gaze on the vast glowing vault of Kroisos only in order to etch it away— leaving exposed the tiny tomb of a poor nameless man content with little things. It is a strange and powerful moment of surrogate expenditure. It is a masterstroke of poetic economy—as Simonides commandeers the whole wealth of Kroisos *in abeyance* to light up the tomb of a man too poor to put his own name on his tombstone.

EXCISION

As a poet who wrote on stone, Simonides had reason to concern himself with the processes of excision, eliding and removal of surface. To carve an inscription on stone is to cut away everything that is not the meaning. Paul Celan was no epigraphic poet yet, in

---

[18] Simonides fr. 80 *FGE; Palatine Anthology* 7.507.

a different way, he found his writing surface had to be modified for use.

His very difficult relationship with the German language is a history of that modification. For although he described German as a language stuffed with falsity and gagged with "the ashes of burned-out meanings,"[19] he nonetheless chose this surface for his poetic work, paring it down to an idiolect that is so extreme a formation it bears about the same relation to standard German as a crystal of granite to a range of hills.

Excision is a topic Celan examines explicitly in a poem of 1964. The poem was composed during a period when he was paying attention to the artwork of his wife, a printmaker, and was collaborating with her on an edition of his poems that would feature eight of her etchings. Of her printing plates he said, "I am very impressed and influenced by the intellectual precision of this."[20] The poem "Weggebeizt" considers his own art under the figure of etching. Here is the first stanza:[21]

WEGGEBEIZT vom
Strahlenwind deiner Sprache
das bunte Gerede des An-
erlebten—das hundert-
züngige Mein-
gedicht, das Genicht.

[Bitten away by the
radiance wind of your language
the manycoloured talk of pasted-
on experience—the hundred-
tongued lie-
poem, the noem.]

The past participle that begins the poem ("Bitten away") may be a technical printmaker's term referring to the biting of acid into the lines on an etching plate, or it may also be a geological verb

---

[19] . . . *die Asche ausgebrannter Sinngebung:* Celan (1990), 10; Waldrop (1986), 6.
[20] Huppert (1988), 136.
[21] Celan (1983), 2:31.

describing the erosion of earth's surface by natural forces. The addressee of the poem ("your language") may be Celan's wife working with her language of acids, or perhaps God working with his language of radiance and wind. In either case, a contrast is drawn between the authenticity of these languages and the imprecise perjury of the verbal art, which is denounced as gossip and lies.[22] Celan didn't like very much twentieth-century poetry, he thought it had no reality in it. He wanted to do something different with words, something that he called "measuring out the area of the given and the possible." His envy of the printmaker's precision parallels Simonides' concern for the physical facts of stone-cutting. Both etching and epigraphy are processes of excision, which seek to construct a moment of attention by cutting away or biting away or eliding away what is irrelevant so as to leave a meaning exposed on the surface. Drastic negation is inherent in the physical act. Celan, like Simonides, had an inclination to take negativity further, to construct a moment of negative attention within words themselves. For example, the neologism that ends the stanza just cited. "Noem" translates German *Genicht*, a word Celan made up possibly out of the noun *Gedicht* ("poem") and the negative adverb *nicht* ("not"). So: "noem," a poem that both is and is not, a verse nothingness, a poeticized negativity. It is a word that makes use of the void to think the full. Like the man who is not Kroisos, it glows with the wealth of a refused truth. From the process of etching we can perhaps derive an analogy for this rich refusal of the "noem."

An etching begins with a drawing on a zinc or copper plate. The drawing is done with a needle or fine-pointed instrument. In order for the lines of the needle to be visible on the plate, whose surface is highly transparent, the ground of the plate is blackened. The etcher therefore makes a drawing of white lines on a black surface—it is an inside-out drawing, a negative design. There is a certain kind of thinking peculiar to negative design. It is the kind of thinking that mystics do when they say, as for exam-

---

22 But the formation *Mein-gedicht* is ambiguous: "my-poem" is just as possible as "lie-poem." See Michael Hamburger's remarks in his introduction to Celan (1988), 26.

ple Meister Eckhart does, "God is not Being. . . . I would be as wrong to call God a Being as I would be to call the sun black."[23] Now an etcher has to learn to draw the sun black so that it will print white. In an interview, Paul Celan referred to this feature of the etching method as "undissembled ambiguity."[24] His own poetic language shows a preoccupation with such ambiguity, with black suns and negative designs and with the dialectic of absence and presence that is implicit in negation. Many scholarly paragraphs have been written on this aspect of his style. But a negative theology may begin as just a way of thinking about the surface on which you are working, whether it is a zinc plate or a slab of stone or the facts of human language. Let us look at a poem in which Celan represents this surface in process.

KEINE SANDKUNST MEHR, kein Sandbuch, keine Meister.

Nichts erwürfelt. Wieviel
Stumme?
Siebenzehn.

Deine Frage—deine Antwort.
Dein Gesang, was weiß er?

Tiefimschnee,
      Iefimnee,
          I - i - e.[25]

[NO MORE SAND ART, no sand book, no masters.

Nothing on the dice. How many
Mutes?
Seven and ten.

Your question—your answer.
Your song, what does it know?

Deepinsnow,
      Eeepinow,
          E - i - o.]

[23] Quint (1936), 1:145.
[24] Felstiner (1995), 232; Huppert (1988), 153.
[25] Celan (1983), 2:39.

A bit of background on this poem. Composed in 1965, a time when Celan was becoming more and more disheartened by the resurgence of anti-Semitism in Europe and also by the deaf ears with which he felt the European literary community listened to his verse, the poem seems to refer in its opening line ("No more sand art, no sand book") to the first book of poetry he published, which was called *Sand from the Urns,* in 1948. The phrase at the end of the opening line ("no masters") is probably a reference to a poem from that early collection that became very famous and was anthologized again and again. This is the poem "Death-fugue," which concerns the concentrationary universe and contains the refrain "Death is a master from Germany." Both the book *Sand from the Urns* and the poem "Deathfugue" were repudiated by Celan himself, the former because of the many misprints that appeared in the text when it was published, the latter because he came to think it spoke too directly or explicitly about things that could not be said.

"Nothing on the dice," says the second line of the poem. This may be another allusion to Celan's own poetic past, specifically to the French poet Mallarmé, whose long poem "A Throw Of The Dice" was much admired and also translated by Celan during his early years in Paris. But by 1965 Celan was no longer imitating Mallarmé and aestheticism in general seemed irrelevant to his project. So the lines "No more sand art, no sand book, no masters. Nothing on the dice . . . " repudiate a kind of art and a stage of himself that no longer suffice; a stage in which he had sought to "poeticize" reality (as he says) rather than simply to "name" it.

I don't know who the seven and ten mutes in the middle are. Their muteness remains, another sort of repudiation.[26]

The poem ends "Deepinsnow." Throughout Celan's work, snow

[26] Critics have raised possibilities. One might see the number as another nod of dismissal to Mallarmé, who fancied numerology; as a count of the kinsmen Celan lost in the war; as part of a paradoxically neat question and answer (paradoxical because the question comes out of nowhere and the answer tells us nothing) representing the sort of empty information often supplied by "song" instead of knowledge. "Maybe seventeen mutes lack one for the central Eighteen Prayer of Judaic liturgy or simply '18' which in Hebrew spells 'alive'" suggests Felstiner (1995), 220. See also Bollack in Colin (1987), 136; Glenn (1973), 143; Jackson

seems to be a figure for the season and the conditions of his mother's death. In between the sand and the snow comes a question (which is also an answer), "Your song, what does it know?" I am inclined to take this as a question addressed by the poet to the poet. He is demanding an epistemology of himself. The whole poem is his answer. It juxtaposes two kinds of song, two ways of knowing. One created by sand art, the other by snow art. What is the difference?

The difference has to do with time. Remember how King Lear, a man whose tragedy is a process of coming to know the price of everything and the value of nothing, greets Cordelia's death by saying the adverb "never" five times.[27] "Never" is a word in which time cuts across our nothingness. But unlike us, a word can be repeated. Unlike us a word can stay. Sand, if you pick it up, will quickly run through your fingers, then lie on the ground inert, possibly for centuries. Snow, if you pick it up, will slowly melt— reduce itself to its essence—then vanish. Sand art works by replication ("No more sand . . . no sand . . . no"). Sand art may represent the entire vast improvident and infinitely replicable burned-out linguistic store of poeticizing poetry. Snow art, on the other hand, keeps a sense of its own economy. Which Celan emphasizes by paring the last word down gradually ("Deepinsnow, Eepinow, E-i-o") to its merest constituent vowels. He permits us to see the name he is giving to reality, then to see it melt away into the different whiteness of the page. Time is present in this whiteness as air inside snow. But suspended within the act of whitening is a terribly quiet pun. For one cannot help but think, watching "Deepinsnow" melt away, that if this poem were translated into Hebrew, a language in which vowels are not usually printed, it would vanish even before its appointed end. As did many a Hebrew.

(1978), 219; Maassen (1972), 199; Petuchowski (1978), 111–36; and cf. "Edgar I nothing am" (*King Lear* 2.3.21).

[27] *King Lear* 5.3.308. "Lear's 'Never never never never never!' marks for him the end of possibilities in time, his temporalizing of the frequent 'nothing' of the tragedy: man is 'nothing' in time": Elton (1988), 106.

In preparing his pun, Celan depends upon a very ancient Hebrew exemplar. It is in the book of *Genesis* (22:17) that God makes Abraham a promise: "That in blessing I will bless thee and in multiplying I will multiply thy seed as the stars of the heaven and as the sand which is upon the sea shore. And thy seed shall possess the gate of his enemies."[28] In his lifetime Celan saw the seed of Abraham lose possession of the gate of his enemies and exchange the innumerability of sand for a specific number that is usually put at six million. By the odd mathematics of that time the number six million came to be equal to zero. Celan sets up a parallel mathematics of reduction, but he has replaced sand with snow and zero with a letter of the alphabet. Here is a short answer to his own epistemological question: what a poet knows is how to imitate the human zero with a poetic "O!" Poetry is an act of memory that carves its way between sand art and snow art, transforming what is innumerable and headed for oblivion into a timeless notation. Excising all that is not grace. But I wonder if Celan is not negating this poetic act even as he executes it, when he turns the last verses of his poem into an inside-out Hebrew lesson: here—unusually—it is the consonants that have to be supplied from memory. Here it is the full that thinks the void. How else to refer to the losses implied in these consonants. Or to the grace that poetry claims as its rate of exchange?

STAR

In Chapter I we began to consider two questions about verbal economy, namely, what exactly is lost to us when words are wasted and where is the human store to which such goods are gathered in? I would like to return to these questions, with consideration of one final stanza of a long poem of Paul Celan called "Engführung" ("The Straitening").[29] This poem is about what happened to Jews in wartime Europe, and the effect of this event on postwar European culture. The effect seems to have been very

---

[28] I owe this reference to Herbert Leibowitz.
[29] Celan (1983), 1:195–202; (1988), 136–49.

little, as Celan sees it. Perhaps nothing. "We put a silence over it," the poem says, describing a half-buried wall on which you can still see the grooves of the bullets where a great number of people were shot. Then comes this stanza:

Also
stehen noch Tempel. Ein
Stern
hat wohl noch Licht.
Nichts,
nichts ist verloren.

[So
there are still temples. A
star
has probably still light.
Nothing,
nothing is lost.]

The sentence "Nothing, nothing is lost" seems to be uttered in a tone of strange irony. Surely not many a Jew believes that although temples and stars still exist, nothing has been lost. But the sentence is also an instance of "undissembled ambiguity." For Nothing is by definition a blank space that has no existence in it, a nullity of Being, something that we as beings cannot experience and could never know. And yet you might say that the universe of the concentration camps, as Celan describes it in the rest of this poem, was a place where people did experience nullity of Being. A world where Nothing itself came forward to be known. An etching plate on which a black sun printed black. And of this world, for these people, it would be true to say that "Nothing is lost" if the essence of Nothing is to not exist.

So an answer to the first question—What is lost when words are wasted?—is simply, "Nothing." But the loss of Nothing is not trivial. As King Lear discovered from Cordelia, "Nothing" is a word that measures out the area of the given and the possible. Once this limit, which should mark Being on the outside edge, has been brought into the center and experienced as ordinary fact, once it

118

has been expended as poeticizing speech, then (in the words of the Fool to his king) "Thou hast pared thy wit o' both sides and left Nothing in the middle." Perhaps Simonides had some such thing in mind when he advised us "to play at life and to be 100 percent serious about Nothing." Perhaps Celan is alluding to it when, throughout his later poetry and nine times in "Engführung," he refers to things that cannot be said by using the printed symbol called an asterisk.[30] Asterisk, that perfectly economical sign. A star in any language. A mark on the page that pulls its own sound in after itself and disappears. A meaning that refuses to waste a single word in order to write itself on the world. Time is present in this refusal. For stars, as you know, exist in their own time. Depending on your coordinates, you may be gazing at a star in the night sky whose actual fire ceased to exist millennia ago. Depending on your alphabet, you may be looking at a word in a poem that has already ended. And still the question remains, Where is the human store to which such economies are gathered in?

[30] On this graphic sign, which appears in other poems of Celan, not to mention those of Mallarmé, see Derrida (1986), 110–15; Fioretos (1994), 322–33; Janz (1976), 223–26; Szondi (1971), 359–78.

All Candled Things

As a child Paul Celan liked to draw burning candles. To capture
with pen and ink the successive phases of flame and extinction
preoccupied him intensely.[1] "I did not love *it*, I loved its burning
down and you know I haven't loved anything since," says his protago-
nist Klein near the end of *Conversation in the Mountains*. To witness
the mortal flame, burning and burning down, is a poet's work. Celan
refers to this work, in a poem written on his birthday in 1967, as:

Lesestationen im Spätwort,

Sparflammenpunkte
am Himmel. . . .[2]

[Reading stations in the late word,

saving flamepoints
in the sky. . . .]

Whom do "saving flamepoints" (*Sparflammenpunkte*) save? Per-
haps themselves. The German verb *sparen* means "to be thrifty."
And *Lesestationen im Spätwort* plays upon the term *Spätlese,* a "late
gleaning" of ripe grapes. Certainly Celan knew better than anyone
how to go about gleaning the word. Yet in the end he despaired of
the task. On the day he took his own life by drowning (April 20,
1970), he left open on his desk a biography of Hölderlin with part
of a sentence underlined:

Sometimes this genius goes dark and sinks down into the well of the
heart.[3]

In a poem written some weeks earlier, he seems to describe his
own sinking down:

[1] Chalfen (1991), 68.
[2] Celan (1983), 2:324.13–15; (1988), 312–13.13–15.
[3] Felstiner (1995), 287.

120

DIE EWIGKEITEN fuhren
ihm ins Gesicht und drüber
hinaus,

langsam löschte ein Brand
alles Gekerzte. . . .[4]

[The eternities drove at
his face and
beyond it,

slowly a fire extinguished
all candled things. . . .]

We cannot assimilate this despair but we should study it. For a poet's despair is not just personal; he despairs of the word and that implicates all our hopes. Every time a poet writes a poem he is asking the question, Do words hold good? And the answer *has to be yes*: it is the contrafactual condition upon which a poet's life depends. We have looked at the ways in which this condition informs ancient Greek attitudes to poets and poetry—built into Homer's blindness and Simonides' avarice, sleepshaped in the story of Danaë, deathcolored on the ship of Theseus, quickchanging as a longwinged fly, sudden as a collapsed roof. We have seen Simonides estranged from his fellows on account of this condition; we have seen him recognize, resent and negotiate his estrangement; we have seen him transform it into a poetic method of luminous and precise economy. We have not seen him despair.

Simonides' lack of despair is noteworthy. Do words hold good for him? Yes they do and, on the basis of this goodness, he invented a genre of poetry.

Epinikion means "upon the occasion of a victory." It is the Greek name for a formal praise poem, or epinician ode, in honor of a victor in the athletic games. The Olympic Games were the most illustrious of these athletic occasions, held at Olympia every four years and attended by people from all over the Greek world. But many other ancient cities (including Delos, Corinth and Nemea)

---

[4] Celan (1983), 2:283.1–5; (1988), 298–99.1–5.

had contests and held festivals to celebrate victors. Epinician odes were part of these celebrations. The odes were given in choral performance—combining music, song and dance—to an audience that might include the victor, his kinsmen, fellow competitors, fellow citizens and other spectators. It would be hard to overestimate the social, ethical and epistemological importance of these performances to the community in which they took place. Indeed community is constituted by such acts. Games are for winners. They stand alone. Community comprises all the rest of us, who do not win, but watch and recognize the victor's separate struggle, finding a way to praise it. Praise poetry addresses itself to an individual who has chosen to test the limits of human possibility and momentarily succeeded. His flame is burning very bright. Looking at it we feel both love and hate. Hate because he has surpassed us, love because his light falls on our hopes, enlarging them. Ancient Greek epinician poets are candid about the natural human ambivalence that greets excellence in other people, and they take seriously their own function of counterbalancing private emotion with communal reasoning. The poet's voice pulls order out of agonistic chaos and forms it into an object of common delight. So Pindar says:

ἐγὼ δ᾽ ἀστοῖς ἁδὼν . . .
αἰνέων αἰνητά, μομφὰν δ᾽ ἐπισπείρων ἀλιτροῖς.[5]

[I cheer my townspeople . . .
because I praise what is praiseworthy
and scatter blame on the unrighteous.]

Pindar's ability to praise and blame depends on the goodness of his words. He has to know the difference between praiseworthy and blameworthy action; he has to name it. This saves the community, like rain, Pindar says:

τέθμιόν μοι φαμὶ σαφέστατον ἔμμεν
τάνδ᾽ ἐπιστείχοντα νᾶσον ῥαινέμεν εὐλογίαις.[6]

[5] Pindar *Nemeans* 8.38–39.
[6] Pindar *Isthmians* 6.20.

[I say it is a necessary and absolutely lucid law
that I come to this island and rain the water of praise on it.]

Now Pindar is certainly the most famous epinician poet of the
Greek tradition. But he was not the first. Tradition ascribes the
invention of this genre to Simonides of Keos. There are fragmen-
tary remains of Simonidean victory odes honoring winners in
sprinting, wrestling, boxing, pentathlon, chariot racing and mule
racing. These pieces are, for the most part, brief and dull. Si-
monides shows but a dim interest in athletes or prizes. The con-
cept of praise itself, however, stirs him profoundly. In a long
poem that is arguably the most difficult of his oeuvre, he enter-
tains the question, Do words of praise hold good? And answers it
with a poetic action—precisely the action we saw recommended
by Paul Celan—he "measures off the area of the given and the
possible":[7]

ἄνδρ᾽ ἀγαθὸν μὲν ἀλαθέως γενέσθαι
χαλεπὸν χερσίν τε καὶ ποσὶ καὶ νόωι
   τετράγωνον ἄνευ ψόγου τετυγμένον·
[   ]

οὐδέ μοι ἐμμελέως τὸ Πιττάκειον
νέμεται, καίτοι σοφοῦ παρὰ φωτὸς εἰ-
   ρημένον· χαλεπὸν φάτ᾽ ἐσθλὸν ἔμμεναι.
θεὸς ἂν μόνος τοῦτ᾽ ἔχοι γέρας, ἄνδρα δ᾽ οὐκ
   ἔστι μὴ οὐ κακὸν ἔμμεναι,
ὃν ἀμήχανος συμφορὰ καθέληι·
πράξας γὰρ εὖ πᾶς ἀνὴρ ἀγαθός,
κακὸς δ᾽ εἰ κακῶς
[ἐπὶ πλεῖστον δὲ καὶ ἄριστοί εἰσιν
οὓς ἂν οἱ θεοὶ φιλῶσιν.]

τοὔνεκεν οὔ ποτ᾽ ἐγὼ τὸ μὴ γενέσθαι
δυνατὸν διζήμενος κενεὰν ἐς ἄ-
   πρακτον ἐλπίδα μοῖραν αἰῶνος βαλέω,
πανάμωμον ἄνθρωπον, εὐρυεδέος ὅσοι
   καρπὸν αἰνύμεθα χθονός·

[7] See above, Chapter III, n. 16.

ἐπὶ δ᾽ ὑμὶν εὑρὼν ἀπαγγελέω·
πάντας δ᾽ ἐπαίνημι καὶ φιλέω,
ἑκὼν ὅστις ἔρδηι
μηδὲν αἰσχρόν· ἀνάγκαι
δ᾽ οὐδὲ θεοὶ μάχονται.

[   ]

[οὐκ εἰμὶ φιλόψογος, ἐπεὶ ἔμοιγε ἐξαρκεῖ
ὃς ἂν μὴ κακὸς ἦι] μηδ᾽ ἄγαν ἀπάλαμνος εἰ-
  δώς γ᾽ ὀνησίπολιν δίκαν,
ὑγιὴς ἀνήρ· οὐδὲ μή μιν ἐγὼ
μωμήσομαι· τῶν γὰρ ἠλιθίων
ἀπείρων γενέθλα.
πάντα τοι καλά, τοῖσίν
τ᾽ αἰσχρὰ μὴ μέμεικται.[8]

---

[8] Simonides fr. 542 *PMG;* Plato *Protagoras* 340A–348A. The text is problematic; there may be missing verses here and there, or passages of paraphrase masquerading as quotation. The possibility has occurred to me that Plato made the poem up. At any rate, it has no separate manuscript tradition, having been preserved for us only in a Platonic conversation between Sokrates and the sophist Protagoras, each of whom uses the poem as material for literary critical exercises of escalating brilliance. Neither Protagoras nor Sokrates seems very interested in what Simonides was really trying to say in his poem; the text is a means to an end for them. But I wonder about the innocence of Plato's editorial choice. Certainly Simonides, held accountable by the Greeks for professionalizing the art of poetry, provides a worthy analogue to Protagoras the sophist, who supported himself by marketing traditional wisdom in prose and invented the trade of the professional educator. Moreoever, both Protagoras and Simonides won for their pains a solid reputation of avarice, penury and greed. Protagoras is reputed to have made more money than Pheidias, the most famous sculptor of his day, or ten other sculptors put together. Plato and others remark on this: like Simonides, the sophist gave people a shock by putting a price on a commodity previously called "wisdom" or "truth." Remember, too, the best known of Protagoras' sayings: "Man is the measure of all things, both of the things that are, that they are, and of the things that are not, that they are not." Simonides would almost certainly have looked upon Protagorean relativism as naive or impious; nonetheless, his own portfolio as an epinician poet (as he establishes it in fr. 542) rests on a strong claim to be able to take the measure of a man. What a happy accident that these two calibrators converge in a Platonic dialogue whose philosophic point is something Sokrates calls "an art of measure that can save your life." History would be a very strange thing if it contained no accidents, Marx reminds us.

[Hard to become truly a good man
in hands and feet and mind
built four-square without blame.

Now if you ask me, the old saying of Pittakos does not
define its terms properly although
said by a wise man: *hard* (he says) *to be good.*
The fact is, God alone could have this privilege.
Man cannot but be bad
if the misfortune machine pulls him down.
Yes sure, every man is good when things are good
and bad when things are bad
(and in general the best are the ones
whom the gods love).

So never shall I go searching after what cannot come into being
anyhow—throwing the space of my life down empty in actionless
    hope—
an All Blameless Man
among those of us who feed on the food of the earth
(but if I find one I'll send you the news).
I praise and love anyone
whoever willingly does
nothing ugly. Necessity
not even gods fight.

No I do not like blaming. Because for me it's enough
if someone is other than bad—not too much out of hand,
conscious at least of the justice that helps the city,
a healthy man. No I shall not
lay blame. Because fools
are a species that never ends.
All things, you know, are beautiful with which
ugly things are not mixed.]

Do words of praise hold good? Yes, Simonides maintains, if a
real poet measures them out. How do we know who is a real poet?
The poet tells us. The commodity that Simonides put on sale when
he invented epinician form, the commodity he is advertising in

125

this poem, is his own unique ability to define the boundaries of human praiseworthiness. He must make us believe in this ability before we can hear his praise. He goes about it (characteristically) by a poetic movement from negative to positive. He sets out all the criteria that do *not* constitute grounds for praise, in order to excise them dramatically and leave his own truth obvious. He excises the legendary sage Pittakos, who failed to draw accurate boundaries (νέμεται, 12) around his concept of the good man. He excises the gods who are simply incommensurable with human boundaries (14, 19–20). He excises the race of fools, who are coextensive with boundlessness (ἀπείρων, 38). What remains is his own measured action of praise and love. "I praise and I love," he says, "whoever willingly does nothing ugly" (27–28).

Simonides' poem is not a poem about good, evil, gods, men or Pittakos so much as it is a poem about Simonides' own epinician necessity, which he establishes in sixteen negative and double-negative formulations, culminating in the ruthless declaration: "All things are beautiful into which ugly things are not mixed." Ruthless because, unless you are one of the species of fools that never ends, you know the human condition is an irretrievably mixed one. All our ambitions submit to this flaw. Our beauties turn base on a dime. We are not four-square. Gods fail to love us. The All Blameless Man turns out not to exist. So where can we go for news of truth? To words. The poet's words remain. His words hold good. In words he knows how to clear away everything ugly, blameworthy, incommensurable or mad and manifest what is worth praise. He can minister to the flame. Gods alone have the power to keep themselves burning. All candled things need a Simonides.

Who needs a Celan? It would be an understatement to say the function of praise is denied to the modern poet. Not only because all epistemological authority to define a boundary between blameworthy and praiseworthy action has been withdrawn from him, but because the justice and health of his community are regarded as beyond redemption. In the ancient view, when clear lines are not drawn between praise and blame, the moral life of the community is confused and befouled; epinician diction typically uses images of darkness, shadow and smoke to represent this condition of social defilement.[9] For example, in this epinician fragment attributed to Simonides:

τό τ]ε καλὸν κρίνει τὸ τ᾽ αἰσχρόν· εἰ δέ
. . . κ]ακαγορεῖ τις ἄθυρον [σ]τόμα
περι]φέρων, ὁ μὲν καπνὸς ἀτελής, ὁ δέ[
χρυ]σὸς οὐ μιαίνετ[α]ι,
ἁ δ᾽] ἀλάθε[ι]α παγκρατής·[10]

[[The poet]
differentiates beautiful from ugly: but . . . if
someone speaks [evil]
broadcasting from a mouth that has no door on it,
the smoke is a blurred and boundless thing.
Yet gold does not become defiled.
And truth is totally strong.]

Simonides associates truth, gold, purity and the ethical discriminations of the poet, over against the "broadcasting" of someone whose evil speech defiles the community like smoke and blurs the real edges of things. Although the fragment is incomplete, we can see its concern to denounce unclarity as an agent of evil and to valorize the praise poet against a background of righteousness. Consider, in contrast, Paul Celan's use of similar raw materials— smoke, gold, purity and the ethical discriminations of the poet— in a poem from 1965 whose standpoint is the antithesis of praise:

ÜPPIGE DURCHSAGE
in einer Gruft, wo
wir mit unsern
Gasfahnen flattern,

---

[9] E.g., Pindar *Nemeans* 1.24–25, 7.61–63.
[10] Simonides fr. 541.1–9 *PMG*. So originally ascribed by Lobel and Turner (1959), 91–94, but the matter remains controversial; Loyd-Jones (1961) and Bowra (1963) argue for Bakkhylidean authorship. See also Donlan (1969); Treu (1960).

127

wir stehen hier
im Geruch
der Heiligkeit, ja.

Brenzlige
Jenseitsschwaden
treten uns dick aus den Poren,

in jeder zweiten
Zahn-
karies erwacht
eine unverwüstliche Hymne.

Den Batzen Zwielicht, den du uns reinwarfst,
komm, schluck ihn mit runter.[11]

[RICH BROADCAST
in a grave, where
we with our
gasflags float,

we stand here
in the odor
of sanctity, yes.

Burnt
beyondsmoke
comes thick from our pores,

in every other
tooth-
cavity awakes
an unravageable hymn.

Two-bit twilight that you tossed in to us,
come, gulp it down too.]

Gold is gone from the mouths of these speakers. Their broadcast
smoke is a deathgas that leaks from every pore, inadvertent blame
of beings befouled in their essence and their history. Clarity, even

---

[11] Celan (1983), 2:192; Felstiner (1995), 235.

of physiological boundaries, is denied them. To differentiate beauty from ugliness is a function no poet could administer here; no ontology of measure can order, cleanse or salvage this community. In fact the poet is absent from the poem until its scathing final sentence, when his subjects of song instruct him to swallow down his own two-bit poetic comment. Truth is not mentioned.

In the ancient world, people inaugurated contests and trials of prowess and strength, like the Olympic Games, to provide a location where human excellence could manifest itself and so become a subject of song, as burning entails flame. Modernity devises different ordeals. Here life and death are not merely analogically present. Burning occurs. Gold is real. Smoke is literal.[12] And it becomes harder (perhaps too hard) for poetry to hold its own. As Simonides once said, "Seeming does violence even to the truth."[13] Do poets still watch the flame burn down? But to praise it is a gratuitous act, like throwing coins onto a pyre.

On the other hand, the economy of the unlost always involves gratuity. Whether you call it a waste of words or an act of grace depends on you. It is typical of Celan (and would have made sense to Simonides) to place at the center of his poem a negative space, the tooth cavity, so that we pay attention to what fills it: *unverwüstliche Hymne,* "unravageable hymn." Is this phrase ironic and more than hopeless? Or does Celan believe of the hymn (what Simonides believes of gold) that it "does not become defiled?"

Celan did not often talk of hymns but he does mention Hölderlin, whose *Hymns* inspired him all his life. The poem he wrote after visiting Hölderlin's tower in Tübingen poses in pure form the question, Do words hold good?[14]

TÜBINGEN, JÄNNER

Zur Blindheit über-
redete Augen.
Ihre—"ein

---

[12] Smoke has a distinct history as symbol, and as degradation of symbol, in Jewish literature: see Fackenheim (1978), 261–63.

[13] Simonides fr. 598 *PMG*, and above.

[14] Celan (1983), 2:226.

Rätsel ist Rein-
entsprungenes"—, ihre
Erinnerung an
schwimmende Hölderlintürme, môwen-
umschwirrt.

Besuche ertrunkener Schreiner bei
diesen
tauchenden Worten:

Käme,
käme ein Mensch,
käme ein Mensch zur Welt, heute, mit
dem Lichtbart der
Patriarchen: er dürfte,
spräch er von dieser
Zeit, er
dürfte
nur lallen und lallen,
immer-, immer-
zuzu.

("Pallaksch. Pallaksch.")

[TÜBINGEN, JANUARY

Eyes talked over
to blindness.
Their—"a
riddle is the purely
originated"—, their
memory of
swimming Hölderlintowers, gull-
whirred.

Visits of drowned joiners to
these
diving words:

Came,
came a man,

130

came a man to the world, today, with
the lightbeard of
the prophets: he could,
if he spoke of this
time, he
could
only stammer and stammer,
over-, over-
againagain.

("Pallaksch. Pallaksch.")]

The poem is a praise of Hölderlin. It begins with his "riddle" and ends with his *Pallaksch*. Both quotations are taken from the world of words that held good for him. "A riddle is the purely originated" comes from his Rhine hymn, and *Pallaksch Pallaksch* is a term he liked to utter in his late years to mean "sometimes yes, sometimes no."[15] He was mad in his late years; you can call *Pallaksch* nonsense. Yet a few pages ago we read and made sense of Celan's admonition, "Keep Yes and No unsplit." A word for "Yes and No" might be useful. Poets keep coming up with these useful inventions; we have seen both Celan and Simonides contructing a word for "Yes and No" out of the operations of the negative, out of the collocation of visibles and invisibles, out of the absent presence of gods in human rooms, out of alchemy, out of memory, out of the rules for elegiac meter and the letters of the Hebrew alphabet, out of strangeness, hospitality, sleep, prayer and commodity exchange. But to be useful, poetic invention has to measure itself against the words that are given and possible, has to tease itself out of the unknown through a language mesh where everything ugly, blameworthy, incommensurable or mad is filtered out. Remarkable how Celan brings Hölderlin through the language mesh, riddle and all.

"A riddle is the purely originated." In its context, this sentence begins the fourth strophe of Hölderlin's *Der Rhein* and can be read backward or forward. Origin as riddle. Riddle as origin. Like

---

[15] According to Hölderlin's biographer, Christoph Theodor Schwab; first noted by Böschenstein (1968), 180.

the source of the Rhine, pure origin is hard to specify. "Even poetry can scarcely unveil it," says the poet. I suspect Celan likes the pun that informs Hölderlin's riddle. His line breaks and word division emphasize the parts of Hölderlin's German word *Rein-entsprungenes,* which means "purely originated" but also sounds like "Rhine-originated" and perhaps even suggests "*Der Rhein-*originated." Pure source, the river Rhine and the poem "Rhine" come together on a point from which rich sense flows. If language were a commerce, punning would be its usury. Aristotle tells us that usury is the most unnatural sort of wealth-getting because it allows money to breed money out of itself instead of being spent as it was intended.[16] Analogously, punning generates an unnatural supplement of significance from a sound that properly expends itself in one meaning alone.

If meaning were expenditure, this riddle would not be cheap. Many a poet or patriarch has paid with his eyes for the privilege of wasting words. Celan implies Hölderlin's place in the tradition with a long repetitive conditional sentence (*Käme . . . zuzu*) that ends in a burst of Hölderlin's private language. Now a private language is a kind of riddle. It raises the same problem of pure origin: you cannot get behind the back of it. *Pallaksch Pallaksch* is its own clue. On the other hand, from Hölderlin's point of view, *Pallaksch Pallaksch* may be an utterance that captures the whole of the truth, purely originated. Celan allows for this possibility when he cites the phrase in brackets—that silent veil he likes to throw around his own riddles. Remember

> (Did you know me,
> hands? I went
> the forked way you showed, my mouth
> spat its gravel, I went, my time
> wandering watches, threw its shadow—did you know me?)

from "Matière de Bretagne"? Remember

> (Were I like you. Were you like me.
> Stand we not

[16] Aristotle *Politics* 1258b.

under *one* tradewind?
We are strangers.)

from "Sprachgitter"? Remember, too, Simonides' Danaë gazing on the face of her infant deep in its purple blanket, mysterious bit of pure origin.

But if to you τὸ δεινόν were τὸ δεινόν,
you would lend your small ear
to what I am saying,

she says. Danaë frames her child in a contrafactual condition that is also a tautology; she seems to stammer. By his face she sees that the child is gone to another world and she does not know its language. Her Greek word τὸ δεινόν can only repeat itself on the surface of his sleep, like someone knocking on silence in search of a sound. Celan frames Hölderlin in a repetitive and ambiguous condition ("If a man came . . . he could only stammer"). This sentence may be contrafactual, it may not. The subjunctive verbs are vaguely futural, yet anchored to the present time in *heute* ("today"). Like Simonides, Celan is measuring off the area within which words hold good. It is a limited area. An unthinkable good. It comes up against silence. Celan searches into the silence. He lays his ear to the border of that other world: here comes a sound from Hölderlin's side. Two sharp knocks. *"Pallaksch. Pallaksch."*

Every praise poem is a presentiment of itself—a neologism that throws itself forward in song to whoever will complete it by seeing and hearing it, by taking it into their mind or heart. A praise poet has to construct fast, in the course of each song, this community that will receive the song. He does so by presuming it already exists and by sustaining a mood of witness that claims to be shared primordially between poet and community but in fact occurs within his words. The witnessing of what is praiseworthy is prior in him to praiseworthy acts, as he is prior to the community that will acclaim him its poet and so invent itself. There is something riddling in this. Whoever we are once invented, he is already there, watching the flame burn down.

His priority is like a private wealth. He administers it unevenly, now lavish, now stingy. Why are neologisms disturbing? If we cannot construe them at all, we call them mad. If we can construe them, they raise troubling questions about our own linguistic mastery. We say "coinages" because they disrupt the economic equilibrium of words and things that we had prided ourselves on maintaining. A new compound word in Celan, for example, evokes something that now suddenly seems real, although it didn't exist before and is attainable through this word alone.[17] It comes to us free, like a piece of new air. And (like praise) it has to prepare for itself an ear to hear it, just slightly before it arrives— has to invent its own necessity. Celan calls such things "breathcoin" (*die Atemmünze*).[18] If breath were coin, the poet might not have drowned. Some people think Celan's death is prefigured in the stammering words of "Tübingen, Jänner," as if he were already there: watching it. He stands at a border of whiteness. Facing away from us. Blind to the color of our sail.

Is blindness a defect?

Not always.

Is stammering a waste of words?

Yes and No.

[17] Neumann (1968), 10.

[18] In the poem "Le Contrescarpe" occur these verses: Brich dir die Atemmünze heraus / aus der Luft um duch und den Baum ("Break the breathcoin out / of the air that is around you and around the tree"): Celan (1983), 1:282.

Bibliography

Alpers, S. 1972. "Ut Pictura Noesis? Criticism in Literary Studies and Art History." *New Literary History* 3: 437–58.

Atkins, J. W. H. 1934. *Literary Criticism in Antiquity: A Sketch of Its Development.* 2 vols. Cambridge, Eng.

Austin, M. M., and P. Vidal-Naquet. 1977. *Economic and Social History of Ancient Greece: An Introduction.* Berkeley.

Austin, R. P. 1938. *The Stoichedon Style in Greek Inscriptions.* Oxford.

Barasch, M. 1987. *Giotto and the Language of Gesture.* Cambridge, Eng.

Baumann, G. 1986. *Erinnerungen an Paul Celan.* Frankfurt.

Bell, J. M. 1978. *"Kimbix Kai Sophos: Simonides in the Ancient Anecdotal Tradition."* Quaderni urbinati di cultura classica 28: 29–86.

Benn, G. 1968. *Gesammelte Werke.* 8 vols. Wiesbaden.

Bergson, H. 1928. *Creative Evolution.* Trans. A. Mitchell. London.

Bertaux, P. 1936. *Hölderlin: Essai de biographie intérieure.* Paris.

Blanchot, M. 1949. *La part du feu.* Paris.

Blank, D. 1985. "Socratics versus Sophists on Payment for Teaching." *Classical Antiquity* 4: 1–49.

Block, H. M. 1991. *The Poetry of Paul Celan.* New York.

Bollack, J. 1986. "Le poème *Sprachgitter* et ses interpretations." In Broda (1986), 89–120.

———. 1987. "Paul Celan sur la langue." In Colin (1987), 113–56.

Böschenstein, B. 1968. "Paul Celan: 'Tübingen, Jänner.'" In *Studien zur Dichtung des Absoluten*, 29–40. Zurich.

Bottomore, T. B. 1963. *Karl Marx: Early Writings.* London.

Bourdieu, P. 1977. *Outline of a Theory of Practice.* Trans. R. Nice. Cambridge, Eng.

———. 1985. "La lecture: Une pratique culturelle." In Chartier (1985), 66–89.

Bowra, M. 1963. "Simonides or Bacchylides?" *Hermes* 91: 257–61.

Brink, C. O. 1971. *Horace on Poetry: The Ars Poetica.* 2 vols. Cambridge, Eng.

Broda, M. 1986. *Contre-jour: Études sur Paul Celan.* Paris.

Brunnsåker, S. 1955. *The Tyrant-Slayers of Kritios and Nesiotes.* Lund.

Bruno, V. J. 1977. *Form and Color in Greek Painting.* New York.

Büchner, G. 1922. *Dantons Tod.* Leipzig.

Burke, E. 1757. *A Philosophical Enquiry into the Origin of Our Idea of the Sublime and Beautiful.* London.

Campbell, D. 1991. *Greek Lyric.* 3 vols. Cambridge, Mass.

Carrière, J. 1962. *Théognis: Poèmes élégiaques.* Paris.

Casale, O. M. 1981. *A Leopardi Reader.* Urbana.

Celan, P. 1983. *Gesammelte Werke.* 5 vols. Frankfurt.

———. 1986. *Paul Celan: Collected Prose.* Trans. R. Waldrop. Riverdale-on-Hudson.

———. 1988. *Poems of Paul Celan.* Trans. M. Hamburger. New York.

———. 1990. *Der Meridian und andere Prosa.* Frankfurt.

Chalfen, I. 1991. *Paul Celan: A Biography of His Youth.* Trans. M. Bleyleben. New York.

Chantraine, P. 1950. "Les verbes grecs signifiant 'lire.'" In *Mélanges Gregoire*, 2: 110–31. Brussels.

Chartier, R. 1985. *Pratiques de la lecture.* Paris.

Christ, G. 1941. *Simonidesstudien.* Zurich.

Cohen, E. 1992. *The Athenian Economy: A Banking Perspective.* Princeton.

Colin, A. 1987. *Argumentum e Silentio: International Paul Celan Symposium.* Berlin.

Compagner, R. 1988. "Reciprocità economica in Pindaro." *Quaderni urbinati di cultura classica* 29: 77–93.

Connor, W. R. 1971. *The New Politicians of Fifth-Century Athens.* Princeton.

Crotty, K. 1982. *Song and Action: The Victory Odes of Pindar.* Baltimore.

Day, J. 1989. "Rituals in Stone." *Journal of Hellenic Studies* 109: 16–28.

De Man, P. 1971. *Blindness and Insight.* Minneapolis.

———. 1989. *Critical Writings, 1953–1978.* Minneapolis.

Derrida, J. 1986. *Shibboleth pour Paul Celan.* Paris.

Detienne, M. 1981. *Les maîtres de vérité dans la Grèce archaïque.* Paris.

Diels, H. 1951. *Die Fragmente der Vorsokratiker.* 6th ed. Ed. W. Kranz. Berlin.

Dihle, A. 1956. *Studien zür griechischen Biographie.* Göttingen.

Donlan, W. 1969. "Simonides fr. 4D and P. Oxy 2432." *Transactions and Proceedings of the American Philological Association* 100: 90–95.

Donnay, G. 1967. "Les comptes de l'Athéna chryséléphantine du Parthenon." *Bulletin de correspondence hellénique* 91: 50–86.

Dorsch, T. S. 1977. *Classical Literary Criticism: Aristotle, Horace, Longinus.* Harmondsworth.

Du Bos, J. B. 1740. *Réflexions critiques sur la poésie et sur la peinture.* Paris.

Edmonds, J. M. 1927. *Lyra Graeca.* 3 vols. London.

Eliot, G. 1965. *Middlemarch.* Harmondsworth.

Elton, W. R. 1988. *King Lear and the Gods.* Lexington, Ky.

Fackenheim, E. 1978. *The Jewish Return into History.* New York.

Felstiner, J. 1995. *Paul Celan: Poet, Survivor, Jew.* New Haven.

Figueira, T. J. 1981. *Aegina: Society and Politics.* New York.

Fink, E., and M. Heidegger. 1979. "Sleep and Dream." In *Heraclitus Seminar, 1966/67*, 137–49. Trans. C. H. Seibert. University, Ala.

Finley, M. I. 1935. "Emporos, Naukleros and Kapelos." *Classical Philology* 30: 320–26.

———. 1953. "Marriage, Sale and Gift in the Homeric World." In *Economy and Society in Ancient Greece*, 94–130. New York.

Fioretos, A. 1994. *Word Traces: Readings of Paul Celan.* Baltimore.

Fitzgerald, W. 1987. *Agonistic Poetry: The Pindaric Mode in Pindar, Horace, Hölderlin and the English Ode.* Berkeley.

Fränkel, H. 1973. *Early Greek Poetry and Philosophy.* Trans. M. Hadas and J. Willis. New York.

Freeman, K. 1946. *The Pre-Socratic Philosophers.* Cambridge, Eng.

Friedländer, P., and H. B. Hoffleit. 1948. *Epigrammata: Greek Inscriptions in Verse from the Beginnings to the Persian Wars.* Berkeley.

Fynsk, C. 1994. "The Realities at Stake in a Poem: Celan's Bremen and Darmstadt Addresses." In Fioretos (1994), 159–85.

Gauthier, P. 1972. *Symbola.* Nancy.

Gay, P. 1988. *Freud: A Life for Our Time.* New York.

Gentili, B. 1988. *Poetry and Its Public in Ancient Greece.* Trans. A. T. Cole. Baltimore.

Gernet, L. 1968. *The Anthropology of Ancient Greece.* Trans. J. Hamilton and B. Nagy. Baltimore.

———. 1981. *Myth, Religion and Society.* Trans. R. Gordon. Cambridge, Eng.

Glenn, J. 1973. *Paul Celan.* New York.

Golb, J. 1988. "Celan and Heidegger: A Reading of 'Todtnauberg.'" *Seminar* 24: 255–68.

Gombrich, E. H. 1968. *Art and Illusion.* Princeton.

Gomme, A. W. 1954. *The Greek Attitude to Poetry and History.* Berkeley.

Gregory, C. A. 1982. *Gifts and Commodities.* London.

Guthrie, W. K. C. 1969. *A History of Greek Philosophy.* 3 vols. Cambridge, Eng.

Gzella, S. 1971. "Problem of the Fee in Greek Choral Lyric." *Eos* 59: 189–202.

Hagstrum, J. 1958. *The Sister Arts.* Chicago.

Hamann, J. G. 1951. *Sämtliche Werke.* 3 vols. Vienna.

Hamburger, M. 1988. *Poems of Paul Celan.* New York.

———. 1990. "Footpath with Logs at the Limit of Language." *The Independent,* 22 Dec., 33.

Hamilton, H. A. 1899. *The Negative Compounds in Greek.* Ph.D. diss., Johns Hopkins University.

Hamilton, R. 1974. *Epinikion: General Form in the Odes of Pindar.* The Hague.

Hands, A. R. 1968. *Charities and Social Aid in Greece and Rome.* London.

Harriott, R. 1969. *Poetry and Criticism before Plato.* London.

Harrison, E. 1902. *Studies in Theognis.* Cambridge, Eng.

Hauvette, A. 1896. *De l'authenticité des épigrammes de Simonide.* Paris.

Hazlitt, W. M. 1844. *Criticism on Art.* London.

Hegel, F. 1953. *Vorlesungen über die Ästhetik.* Ed. H. Glockner. Stuttgart.

Heidegger, M. 1949. *Existence and Being.* Trans. D. Scott. Chicago.

———. 1962. *Was heisst Denken?* Tübingen.

———. 1971. *Poetry, Language, Thought.* Trans. A. Hofstadter. New York.

———. 1981. *Erläuterungen zu Hölderlins Dichtung.* Frankfurt.

Heinimann, F. 1945. *Nomos und Physis.* Basel.

Herman, G. 1987. *Ritualized Friendship and the Greek City.* Cambridge, Eng.

Hermeren, G. 1969. *Representation and Meaning in the Visual Arts: A Study of the Methodology of Iconography and Iconology.* Lund.

Hewitt, W. W. 1927. "The Terminology of 'Gratitude' in Greek." *Classical Philology* 22: 142–61.

Hoffman, E. 1925. *Die Sprache und die archaische Logik.* Tübingen.

Hollander, B. 1988. *Translating Tradition: Paul Celan in France.* San Francisco.

Holt, E. G. 1957. *A Documentary History of Art.* 2 vols. Garden City, N.Y.

Horowitz, A. 1985. *You Can Be Your Own Rabbi Most of the Time: A Comprehensive Guide To Jewish Thought, Law, Custom, and Way of Life.* Toronto.

Humphreys, S. 1978. *Anthropology and the Greeks.* London.

Huppert, H. 1988. "'In the Prayer Mill's Rattling': A Visit with Paul Celan." In Hollander (1988): 132–55.

Jackson, J. 1978. *La question du moi: Un aspect de la modernité poétique européene.* Neuchatel.

Jacoby, F. 1945. "Some Athenian Epigrams from the Persian Wars." *Hesperia* 14: 157–211.

Jaeger, W. 1945. *Paideia.* 3 vols. New York.

Janz, M. 1976. *Vom Engagement absoluter Poesie: Zur Lyrik und Ästhetik Paul Celans.* Frankfurt.

Joris, P. 1995. *Paul Celan Breathturn.* Los Angeles.

Jung, C. G. 1953. *Psychology and Alchemy.* Princeton.

Kahn, C. H. 1979. *The Art and Thought of Heraclitus.* Cambridge, Eng.

Kassel, R. 1975. "Names in Verse." *Zeitschrift für Papyrologie und Epigraphie* 19: 211–18.

Kege, W. J. H. F. 1962. *Simonides.* Groningen.

Kelletat, A. 1970. "Accessus zu Celans 'Sprachgitter.'" In Meinecke (1970), 11–48.

Kerferd, G. 1981. *The Sophistic Movement.* Cambridge, Eng.

Keuls, E. 1975. "Skiagraphia Once Again." *American Journal of Archaeology* 79: 1–16.

———. 1978. *Plato and Greek Painting.* Leiden.

Kirk, G. S. 1954. *Heraclitus, The Cosmic Fragments.* Cambridge, Eng.

Klemperer, V. 1995. *Ich will Zeugnis ablegen bis zum letzten: Tagebücher, 1933–1941* and *1942–1945.* Ed. W. Nowojoski and H. Klemperer. Berlin.

Knox, B. M. W. 1968. "Silent Reading in Antiquity." *Greek, Roman and Byzantine Studies* 9: 421–35.

Kraay, C. M. 1964. "Hoards, Small Change and the Origin of Coinage." *Journal of Hellenic Studies* 84: 76–91.

————. 1976. *Archaic and Classical Greek Coins.* Berkeley.

Kroll, J. H., and N. M. Waggoner. 1984. "Dating the Earliest Coins of Athens, Corinth, and Aegina." *American Journal of Archaeology* 88: 325–40.

Kurke, L. 1991. *The Traffic in Praise: Pindar and the Poetics of Social Economy.* Ithaca, N.Y.

————. 1995. "Herodotus and the Language of Metals." *Helios* 22: 36–63.

Lacoue-Labarthe, P. 1986. *La poésie comme expérience.* Paris.

Lattimore, R. 1962. *Themes in Greek and Latin Epitaphs.* Urbana.

Lee, R. W. 1940. "Ut Pictura Poesis." *The Art Bulletin* 23: 197–269.

Lessing, G. E. 1766. *Laokoon: Oder über die Grenzen der Malerie und Poesie.* Berlin.

Letoublon, F. 1995. "Said over the Dead." *Arethusa* 28: 1–20.

Lifshitz, M. 1938. *The Philosophy of Art of Karl Marx.* Trans. R. B. Winn. New York.

Lloyd-Jones, H. 1961. "The Oxyrhynchus Papyri." *Classical Review* 11: 19–23.

Lobel, E., and E. G. Turner. 1959. *The Oxyrhynchus Papyri,* Part 25. London.

Loraux, N. 1986. *The Invention of Athens.* Trans. A. Sheridan. Cambridge, Mass.

Löw, O. 1908. *Charis.* Diss. University of Marburg.

Löwith, K. 1993. *Max Weber and Karl Marx.* Trans. B. S. Turner. London.

Lukács, G. 1917. "Die Subjekt-Objekt Beziehung in der Ästhetik." *Logos* (1917–18): 14–28.

Luther, W. 1935. *Wahrheit und Lüge im ältesten Griechentum.* Borna-Leipzig.

Lyon, J. K. 1971. "Paul Celan and Martin Buber: Poetry as Dialogue." *Proceedings of the Modern Language Association* 86: 110–20.

————. 1974. "Paul Celan's Language of Stone: The Geology of the Poetic Landscape." *Colloquia Germanica* 8: 298–317.

Maassen, J. P. J. 1972. "TiefimSchnee: Zur Lyrik Paul Celans." *Neophilologus* 55: 195–208.

MacLachlan, B. 1993. *The Age of Grace: Charis in Early Greek Poetry.* Princeton.

Mallarmé, S. 1945. *Oeuvres complètes.* Paris.

———. 1977. *The Poems.* Trans. K. Bosley. Middlesex.

Marcovich, M. 1967. *Heraclitus editio maior.* Merida.

Markiewicz, H. 1987. "Ut Pictura Poesis . . . A History of the Topos and the Problem." *Proceedings of the Modern Language Association* 12: 534–56.

Marx, K. 1867. *Das Kapital.* 3 vols. Hamburg.

———. 1939. *Grundrisse der Kritik der Politischen Ökonomie.* Moscow.

———. 1967. *Capital.* Trans. S. Moore and E. Aveling. New York.

———. 1973. *Grundrisse: Foundations of the Critique of Political Economy.* Trans. M. Nicolaus. New York.

Mauss, M. 1925. *Essai sur le don, forme archaïque de l'échange.* Paris.

———. 1967. *The Gift: Forms and Functions of Exchange in Archaic Societies.* Trans. I. Cunnison. New York.

Mayer, P. 1973. "Alle Dichter sind Juden: Zur Lyrik Paul Celans." *Germanisch-Romanische Monatsschrift* 54: 2–37.

McLellan, D. M. 1977. *Karl Marx: Selected Writings.* Oxford.

McLuhan, M. 1968. *Through the Vanishing Point: Space in Poetry and Painting.* New York.

McMahon, A. P. 1956. *Leonardo da Vinci: Treatise on Painting.* Princeton.

Meinecke, D. 1970. *Über Paul Celan.* Frankfurt.

Meiss, M. 1960. *Giotto and Asissi.* New York.

Meritt, B. D. 1936. "Greek Inscriptions." *Hesperia* 5:355–441.

Milne, J. G. 1938. *The First Stages of the Development of Greek Coinage.* Oxford.

Momigliano, A. 1971. *The Development of Greek Biography.* Cambridge, Mass.

Morris, I. 1986. "Gift and Commodity in Ancient Greece." *Man.* 21: 1–17.

Most, G. W. 1985. *The Measures of Praise: Structure and Function in Pindar's Second Pythian and Seventh Nemean.* Göttingen.

Nagele, R. 1987. "Paul Celan: Konfigurationen Freuds." In Colin (1987), 237–72.

Nagy, G. 1983. "*Sema* and *Noesis:* Some Illustrations." *Arethusa* 16: 35–55.

Nestle, W. 1942. *Vom Mythos zum Logos.* Stuttgart.

Neumann, P. N. 1968. *Zur Lyric Paul Celans.* Göttingen.

Nisetich, F. 1975. *Pindar's Victory Songs.* Baltimore.

Olsson, A. 1994. "Spectral Analysis: A Commentary on 'Solve' and 'Coagula.'" In Fioretos (1994), 267–79.

Page, D. L. 1962. *Poetae Melici Graeci.* Oxford.

———. 1981. *Further Greek Epigrams.* Oxford.

Panofsky, E. 1939. *Studies in Iconology.* Oxford.

Park, R. 1969. "*Ut Pictura Poesis:* The Nineteenth Century Aftermath." *Journal of Aesthetics and Art Criticism* 28: 155–69.

Peristiany, J. G. 1966. *Honour and Shame: The Values of Mediterranean Society.* Chicago.

Petuchowski, E. 1978. "A New Approach to Paul Celan's 'Argumentum e Silentio.'" *Deutsche Vierteljahresschrift für Literaturwissenschaft und Geistesgeschichte* 52: 11–136.

Pilling, G. 1980. *Marx's Capital.* London.

Pöggeler, O. 1986. *Spur des Worts.* Munich.

Pohlenz, M. 1920. "Die Anfange der griechischen Poetik." *Göttingen Nachrichten* 4: 162–78.

Polanyi, K. 1957. *Trade and Markets in the Ancient Empires.* Chicago.

———. 1968. *Primitive, Archaic and Modern Economies: Essays of Karl Polanyi.* New York.

Pollitt, J. J. 1963. *The Critical Terminology of the Visual Arts in Ancient Greece.* Ph.D. diss., Columbia University.

———. 1965. *The Art of Greece.* Englewood Cliffs, N.J.

———. 1974. *The Ancient View of Greek Art.* New Haven.

Prier, R. A. 1978. "Sema and the Symbolic Nature of Pre-Socratic Thought." *Quaderni urbinati di cultura classica* 29: 91–101.

Quint, J. 1936. *Meister Eckharts Predignten.* 4 vols. Stuttgart.

Radermacher, L. 1951. *Artium Scriptores (Reste der voraristotelischen Rhetorik).* Abh. 3 in *Wien. Sitzb.* CCXXVII. Vienna.

Raubitschek, A. E. 1968. "Das Denkmal-Epigram." In *L'épigramme grecque,* Fondation Hardt, Entretiens 14: 4–52. Vandoeuvres-Genève.

Richter, G. M. 1929. *The Sculpture and Sculptors of the Greeks.* New Haven.

Rilke, R. M. 1963. *Sämtliche Werke.* 4 vols. Wiesbaden.

Robertson, M. 1959. *Greek Painting.* Geneva.

Robinson, T. M. 1979. *Contrasting Arguments: An Edition of the Dissoi Logoi.* New York.

———. 1987. "Plato, Heraclitus and Greek Poetry." In *Greek Tragedy and Its Legacy: Essays Presented to D. J. Conacher.* Ed. M. Cropp, E. Fantham, and S. E. Scully. Calgary.

Rose, H. J. 1923. "The Speaking Stone." *Classical Review* 37: 162–63.

Rose, S. 1993. *The Making of Memory.* London.

Rosenmeyer, T. G. 1965. "Gorgias, Aeschylus, and *Apate.*" *American Journal of Philology* 76: 225–60.

Rostagni, A. 1922. "Aristotele e Aristotelismo." *Studia italiana* 2: 55–79.

Sahlins, M. 1972. *Stone Age Economics.* Chicago.

Sartre, J-P. 1988. *Mallarmé or the Poet of Nothingness.* Trans. E. Sturm. London.

Schapiro, M. 1973. *Words and Pictures: On the Literal and the Symbolic in the Illustration of a Text.* The Hague.

———. 1977. *Selected Papers.* New York.

Schulz, G-M. 1977. *Negativität in der Dichtung Paul Celans.* Tübingen.

Snell, B. 1926. "Die Sprache Heraklits." *Hermes* 61: 368–77.

Sohn-Rethel, A. 1978. *Intellectual and Manual Labour: A Critique of Epistemology.* London.

Spector, N. B. 1973. *The Romance of Tristan and Isolt.* Evanston.

Spence, J. D. 1985. *The Memory Palace of Matteo Ricci.* Boston.

Starr, C. G. 1970. *Athenian Coinage.* Oxford.

———. 1977. *The Economic and Social Growth of Early Greece, 800–500 B.C.* Oxford.

Struik, D. J. 1964. *Economic and Philosophic MSS of 1844 by Karl Marx.* Trans. M. Milligan. New York.

Sullivan, M. 1980. *The Three Perfections.* New York.

Suss, W. 1910. *Ethos: Studien zur alteren griechischen Rhetorik.* Leipzig.

Svenbro, J. 1976. *La parole et le marbre.* Lund.

———. 1988. *Phrasikleia: Anthropologie de la lecture en Grèce ancienne.* Paris.

Swindler, M. 1929. *Ancient Painting.* New Haven.

Szondi, P. 1971. "Lecture de Strette: Essai sur la poésie de Paul Celan." *Critique* 27: 356–79.

Taylor, F. S. 1930. "A Survey of Greek Alchemy." *Journal of Hellenic Studies* 50: 109–40.

Taylor, M. N. 1981. *The Tyrant Slayers: The Heroic Image in the Fifth Century B.C.* New York.

Thayer, H. S. 1975. "Plato's Quarrel with Poetry: Simonides." *Journal of the History of Ideas* 36: 1–26.

Thesloff, H. 1961. *Introduction to the Pythagorean Writings of the Hellenistic Period.* Abo.

Thompson, H. A. 1957. *The Athenian Agora,* Vol. 3, *Literary and Epigraphical Evidence.* Princeton.

Thompson, H. A., and R. E. Wycherly. 1972. *The Athenian Agora,* Vol. 14, *The History, Shape, and Uses of an Ancient City Center.* Princeton.

Tod, M. N. 1946–48. *A Selection of Greek Historical Inscriptions.* 2 vols. Oxford.

Treu, M. 1960. "Neues zu Simoides (P. Ox. 2432)." *Rheinisches Museum* 103: 319–36.

Trimpi, W. 1973. "The Meaning of Horace's *Ut Pictura Poesis.*" *Journal of the Warburg and Courtauld Institutes* 36: 1–34.

Trost, H. 1964. *Giotto.* Berlin.

Turner, V. 1974. *Dramas, Fields, and Metaphors: Symbolic Action in Human Society.* Ithaca, N.Y.

Untersteiner, M. 1949. *Sofisti, Testimonianze e Frammenti.* 2 vols. Florence.

Uspensky, B. A. 1972. "Structural Isomorphism of Verbal and Visual Art." In *Poetics: International Review for the Theory of Literature.* The Hague.

Van Groningen, B. A. 1948. "Simonide et les Thessaliens." *Mnemosyne* 1: 1–7.

Van Hook, L. R. 1905. *The Metaphorical Terminology of Greek Rhetoric and Literary Criticism.* Chicago.

Van Raalte, M. 1986. *Rhythm and Metre: Towards A Systematic Description of Greek Versification.* Assen/Maastricht, The Netherlands.

Wade-Gery, H. T. 1933. "Classical Epigrams and Epitaphs." *Journal of Hellenic Studies* 53: 71–104.

Waldrop, R. 1986. *Paul Celan: Collected Prose.* Riverdale-on-Hudson.

Wallace, M. B. 1984. "The Metres of Early Greek Epigram." In *Greek Poetry and Philosophy: Studies In Honour of L. E. Woodbury.* Ed. D. E. Gerber. Chico, Calif.

Washburn, K., and M. Guillemin. 1986. *Paul Celan: Last Poems.* San Francisco.

Webster, T. B. L. 1939. "Greek Theories of Art and Literature." *Classical Quarterly* 33: 149–71.

Wellek, R. 1942. "The Parallelism between Literature and the Arts." In *English Institute Annual 1941,* New York. 53–70.

West, M. L. 1971. *Iambi et Elegi Graeci.* 2 vols. Oxford.

Wilamowitz-Moellendorf, U. von 1913. *Sappho und Simonides.* Berlin.

———. 1922. *Pindar.* Berlin.

Wimsatt, W. K. 1954. *The Verbal Icon.* Lexington, Ky.

Wolfe, T. 1975. *The Painted Word.* New York.

Woodbury, L. 1953. "Simonides on *Arete.*" *Transactions and Proceedings of the American Philological Association* 84: 135–63.

———. 1968. "Pindar and the Mercenary Muse." *Transactions and Proceedings of the American Philological Association* 99: 527–42.

Woodhead, W. 1959. *The Study of Greek Inscriptions.* Cambridge, Eng.

Yates, F. 1966. *The Art of Memory.* New York.

Index